Reinventing Organizations

An Illustrated Invitation to Join the Conversation
on Next-Stage Organizations

Published by Nelson Parker.

Cover design: Véronique Geubelle.

Printed on paper from SFI (USA) or FSC Mix (UK) certified sources using water-based inks.

Praise for the original edition of Reinventing Organizations

"A stimulating and inspiring read!"

Robert Kegan, Harvard University's Meehan Professor of Adult Learning and author of *In Over Our Heads*

"Everything you need to know about building a new paradigm organization!"

Richard Barrett, chairman and founder of the Barrett Values Centre

"Congratulations on a spectacular treatise."

Ken Wilber, author of *A Brief History of Everything*

"Ground-breaker! Game-changer! Brilliant!"

Jenny Wade, Ph.D., author of *Changes of Mind*

"Frederic Laloux has done business people and professionals everywhere a signal service."

Bill Torbert, author of *Action Inquiry*

"The most important and inspiring business book I've ever read."

Tony Schwartz, author of *The Way We're Working Isn't Working*

"A book like *Reinventing Organizations* only comes along once in a decade."

Norman Wolfe, author of *The Living Organization*

"Frederic Laloux is one of the few management leaders exploring what comes next. It's deeply different."

Bill Drayton, founder, Ashoka: Innovators for the Public

7 INTRODUCTION
This doesn't quite look like a management book

13 PART 1
Could we be about to invent a whole
new management paradigm?

41 PART 2
How do these new organizations work, then?

57 Self-management

81 Wholeness

111 Evolutionary purpose

133 PART 3
So... how do we get there?

INTRODUCTION

This doesn't quite look
like a management book

Many people seem truly inspired to hear that a whole new kind of organization is emerging

... but not everyone has time to read a 360-page management book about it.

Reinventing Organizations is one of those rare books that has become a true word-of-mouth phenomenon. Its hopeful message that we can build radically more powerful, soulful, and purposeful organizations has resonated with readers all around the world.

The most amazing things have started happening. Readers in many countries spontaneously reached out to publishers to insist on a translation. Two readers in Chile decided not to wait and paid for a translation themselves, and so did a reader in Ukraine for a Russian translation. Someone in the US bought himself a home studio to record an audio version. Other readers are busy creating a computer game from the book, and an increasing number of university professors have integrated the book into the curriculum of their business schools. As a result of all this momentum, I'm hearing from lots and lots of organizations, large and small, that have committed to fundamentally reinvent themselves.

That so many people resonate with the book has to do, I believe, with the fact that almost everyone today feels that something is broken in our organizations. We can all tell sad stories of how management, as we practice it today, drains life and energy out of the workplace: organizations where bureaucracy has taken over; workplaces fraught with ego trips and power games, infighting, and silos; organizations where people at the top make decisions that leave people below scratching their heads in bewilderment, if not outright frustration …

A great number among us yearn for something more and resonate with the hopeful message that a better way to run businesses and nonprofits, schools and hospitals is emerging.

But—can you believe it?—I've been told not everyone wants to read a whole management book about it. A reader suggested that I add illustrations to my book, and she introduced me to Etienne, a wonderfully gifted illustrator who has become a friend. That's when the idea emerged not just to add a few illustrations to the existing book, but to create a new one—an illustrated, introductory version to the ideas of *Reinventing Organizations*!

What this book is

A lively introduction to the main ideas of *Reinventing Organizations* that you can read almost in one sitting. It's a book you can easily share with other people. A book that helps shift the conversation from what's broken to what's possible. A book that shares how some companies have found ways to be truly powerful, soulful, and purposeful ... and that invites you to imagine a new future for your own organization.

What this book is not

An exhaustive handbook of new management practices. This book highlights a few of the critical elements of the new organizational model that is emerging, just enough, I believe, for you to get a really good sense of what it's all about. It is a shorter but not a dumbed-down version of the original. Just like the original, it might well shake some deep-held assumptions you have about life, about people, and about work. Be prepared for some real food for thought!

A few words about the research

The insights of the book *Reinventing Organizations* are based on three years of research into pioneering organizations. I've screened and studied around fifty organizations in many different sectors and geographies. When it came to selecting a number of these organizations for research in greater depth, I found that quite stringent selection criteria were needed if I wanted the findings to be meaningful.

I decided that I would research organizations in depth

 whatever their *geography*, whether *for profit or nonprofit*, whatever their *industry*,

 but only if they had been operating *for at least five years*, with a *minimum of one hundred employees*, and with a *significant number of management practices that were consistent with the Teal level of consciousness* (more about "Teal" soon).

At first I was afraid I wouldn't find any organizations satisfying these criteria. After all, I was looking at a field that is still very much emerging. Could it be that the most interesting companies would be too small or too recent to draw any meaningful insights? I was relieved that my concerns proved unfounded. Twelve organizations made the cut, and they often far exceeded the criteria. Many have been operating on breakthrough principles for a long time, sometimes thirty years or more, and not just with a few hundred, but sometimes several thousand employees or even tens of thousands of employees.

Research questions and data-gathering methods

The research methodology for these twelve organizations involved studying forty-five fundamental organizational structures and practices (For instance: How does this organization make decisions? How does information flow? How are people evaluated? How do they go about budgeting? Targets? ... Readers interested in the full list of research questions can refer to Appendix 1 in the book *Reinventing Organizations*.) The data-gathering process involved studying all publicly available material, obtaining internal documents, and interviewing organizational founders and leaders through Skype, by phone, or in person, as well as making on-site observations whenever relevant and possible.

PART 1

The way we run organizations today is broken

Could we be about to invent a whole new way?

Something is broken in today's organizations

Somehow, almost everyone senses that the way we run organizations today no longer works for us, that the system has been stretched beyond its limits. It feels sometimes as if everyone is drawing the short straw.

Survey after survey shows that the vast majority of **employees** are disengaged at work. A 2013 Gallup poll, for instance, found that only 13 percent of employees worldwide are engaged at work (63 percent are not engaged and 24 percent are actively disengaged). Management guru Gary Hamel rightly calls this "the shame of management."

Leaders in large organizations seem all-powerful, and, like all of us, they want to look like their life is in control, like they are winners in the game of success. But anyone who has had a chance to have intimate conversations with organizational leaders knows that behind the façade, almost all of them are tired—tired of the rat race and the pressure, the never-ending stream of emails, meetings, and PowerPoint documents. Tired of trying to make people happy, to motivate employees and achieve results. And perhaps most of all, tired of suppressing the nagging questions …

… Is this really what I wanted? Sure I'm successful, but what's the meaning of it all? Is it worth all the sacrifices I've had to make?

Customers' trust in businesses is at an all-time low, and so is their brand loyalty. In many countries, the health care system feels profoundly broken. Children in schools are churned through a fixed curriculum like widgets in a factory, in batches of twenty or thirty at a time, with a shocking proportion discarded by the system along the way.

Perhaps more fundamental than all this is the harm we do to the **planet** that hosts us: to varying degrees, all of our organizations are participating in a system that is polluting the atmosphere, water, and land; destroying invaluable ecosystems and species at a frightening rate; and exhausting raw materials that might never be available again to the children of our children.

It's not just the "corporate" world that is broken

Corporations get much of the blame these days for their greed and their remorseless quest for more profits and growth. But the managerial breakdown affects all types of organizations. From all we know, despite their noble purpose, nonprofits don't make better employers. Nor do government agencies. Nurses leave hospitals in droves because we've turned hospitals into soulless factories. And teachers desert their field of vocation in massive numbers because we have come to worship a cold, mechanical approach to teaching that fails to nourish the souls of either teachers or students. That even people who have chosen their work out of a deep sense of vocation walk out disillusioned has much to say about how deeply dispiriting our management approaches have become.

This might sound surprising, but I think there is reason to be deeply hopeful.

The pain we feel is the pain of something old that is dying ...

... while something new
is waiting to be born.

Humanity evolves by sudden leaps

The historians, philosophers, and psychologists who have studied human evolution all pretty much agree: for some reason, humanity evolves not continuously, but by sudden leaps. And they roughly agree on the major leaps we have had in the course of history.[1] We have been through the tribal age, the age of agriculture, the scientific/industrial age, and so forth. Ken Wilber, a philosopher of human consciousness, refers to these stages using colors, which makes things easy to remember, and I borrowed his color scheme for the book *Reinventing Organizations*.

At every stage, everything changes!

Every stage has brought a breakthrough in terms of technology and the means of subsistence, the power structures that rule society, the religious or spiritual outlook, and many other factors.

One aspect has been mostly overlooked: at every stage, we have also had a breakthrough in the ways we collaborate; with every leap, we have invented a dramatically more powerful "organizational model."

A lot of evidence suggests that we are about to make a new leap ...

... A leap to a stage that Wilber gives the color "Teal" and that I sometimes call "Evolutionary." If there is much pain in the world today, it's in part because our current ways of being in the world feel increasingly outdated and incapable of dealing with the challenges we are facing. We happen to be in one of these transition periods where the old is starting to break down, but the new hasn't taken shape yet. In these confusing times, some people double down on their existing perspectives and beliefs, trying to apply outdated solutions ever more frantically. Others, in increasing numbers, make the leap to a new perspective that allows them to seek solutions that were previously unavailable.

Viewed in this light, it's not extraordinary to think that we might be about to invent a whole new management paradigm

To say that a whole new organizational model might be emerging right now might sound audacious. Is it really possible to invent a whole new management paradigm? And yet, from a historical perspective, this wouldn't be extraordinary at all. It would simply be one more step on the evolutionary staircase.

I believe it's important that we spend just a bit of time with this historical perspective. If you are one of the people who feels that it must be possible, somehow, to run organizations in radically more powerful, soulful, purposeful ways, then you're going to encounter many people who will dismiss this as wishful thinking. They'll try to convince you that what you have in mind is naïve and can't be done.

Well, it turns out that it absolutely can be done—there are a number of truly outstanding organizations that *already* operate from the next stage. But many people, even when they are told about these organizations, are still tempted to dismiss them because they make little sense from today's mainstream perspective. This is what happens at every historical juncture. Imagine what it must have been like three hundred years ago when some people started claiming that a country could be governed with elected representatives instead of a king and a ruling class of aristocrats. They saw what would emerge with clarity, and yet they certainly faced much disbelief.

RED (impulsive) worldview

Let's go on a whirlwind tour of the history of societies and organizations! For tens of thousands of years, people lived in clans of a few dozen or a few hundred people at most. These clans had respected elders, but there was no chief, no hierarchy, and no meaningful division of labor. And thus, no "organizations" to speak of.

And then, starting about ten thousand years ago, we entered a new stage (Impulsive-Red).[2] Societies with several thousand people appeared. To deal with this whole new level of complexity, the role of the chief emerged to enforce social order, through brutal force if needed. We know from research that people at this stage operate in a pretty impulsive and egocentric manner. They haven't internalized rules yet, and it is critical for someone to enforce order from the top. In this worldview, everything is seen through the lens of power.

Either you are more powerful, and you subject the other person to your authority—

—or you are less powerful, and you show allegiance to the boss, who now has some obligation to take care of you.

Today we are easily appalled at Red's crude use of power, and we may overlook the heroic, initiatory, pioneering quality this stage brought to the human journey. Tribes broke out of their usual habitats, exploring new territory. Younger people could shake off the stifling perspective of the elders when a situation called for something new. There is no ambitious taking of initiative, no entrepreneurship without the willful energy that emerged with the Red stage.

Red organizations
are like wolf packs

The glue of Red organizations is the loyalty and the fear the chief inspires to keep the foot soldiers in line. If he shows signs of weakness, or if he becomes too greedy and neglects his duty to take care of his underlings, chances are someone will try to topple him, just like young wolves are said to topple an aging alpha-male.[3] These organizations tend to be unstable and don't scale well, but they are highly entrepreneurial and reactive in chaotic environments.

Archetype: Mafia, Street gang

Historically, the first Red "organizations" emerged when tribes organized to attack and subdue neighboring tribes. Today's archetypical Red organizations are the Mafia or a drug-dealing street gang. More ordinary examples are the many small enterprises where founder-bosses do whatever it takes to succeed and get involved in everything, heedless of structures or processes that would constrain their ability to get things done.

division of labor   **top-down authority**

Two key breakthroughs

Red organizations came with two extraordinary breakthroughs: the division of labor and top-down authority. These breakthoughs can leave us with a bit of a bad taste today. But historically speaking, they were major innovations that allowed groups working together to deal with unprecedented levels of complexity.

AMBER (conformist) worldview

Starting around 4000 BC in Mesopotamia, a more complex worldview arose.[4] It facilitated the leap from a world of proto-empires to the age of agriculture, states and empires, bureaucracies and organized religions.

Agrarian societies are highly stratified in social classes or castes. They are all based on some founding mythology, with God-given, immutable rules of what is right and what is wrong. People at this stage have learned to control Red's impulsiveness—they have internalized rules and exercise self-discipline in service of a common belief. Guilt and shame are the glue of society, and people spend much energy trying to fit in, wearing the right clothes, doing what's expected, thinking the right thoughts.

Surveys show that large parts of the adult population today operate from this stage, although they do so within many belief systems: a right-wing Christian fundamentalist and a left-wing trade union leader might come to opposite conclusions on almost every issue, and yet they could both operate from the Conformist-Amber world of certainties.

Play by the rules, and you are "saved" and become part of the group. Flout the rules, and you are forever rejected, excommunicated.

An archetype of an Amber organization? The army or the Catholic Church

Amber organizations have clear ranks that stack up in a hierarchical pyramid. The foot soldier, the sergeant, the lieutenant, the colonel, the general. The humble priests below the bishops, the archbishops, the cardinals, and, alone at the very top, the pope. Amber organizations live in a world of stability and certainty. Everyone knows what is expected in their role. Stable rituals and processes make life predictable for everyone.

Breakthrough 1:
Replicable processes

Amber organizations, like agrarian societies, rely on stable and replicable processes. Next year's harvest will be based on the same template as this year's and last year's. With stable processes in place, critical knowledge no longer depends on a particular person; it is embedded in the organization. Any person can be replaced—even the pope—and the organization will continue operating seamlessly.

Breakthrough 2:
Stable organization chart

Amber organizations have invented formal job titles, job descriptions, and reporting lines. Thinking happens at the top, execution at the bottom. People at all levels identify with their role, with their "box" in the organization chart. A priest no longer secretly schemes to backstab the bishop to take his place. This has allowed Amber organizations to reach previously unthinkable scales (sending missionaries to the other side of the globe, for instance) and achieve unprecedented results. (Amber organizations built irrigation systems, pyramids, and cathedrals that could never have been contemplated in the previous stage.)

Current examples

Many armies, religious institutions, government agencies, public school systems, and universities are still run today along the lines of Amber organizations. They often operate on the hidden assumption that there is one right way of doing things, that the world is (or should be) immutable, and that lifelong employment should be the norm. When the world changes, they find it hard to accept the need to change and adapt.

ORANGE (achievement) worldview

This is the worldview of the scientific and industrial revolutions.[5] At this stage, the world is no longer seen as a fixed universe governed by immutable rules of right and wrong. Instead, it is seen as a complex clockwork, whose inner workings and natural laws can be investigated and understood. If I'm faster, smarter, more innovative than others in understanding and manipulating the world, I'll achieve more success, wealth, profits, market share, or whatever else I desire. A defining mantra of this perspective states that you can be anyone you want to be, you can achieve anything you set your mind to.

Piaget, the child psychologist, has given us a defining experiment for Orange cognitive thinking: A person is given three glasses of transparent liquid and told that they can be mixed in a way that will produce a yellow color. People that operate with Amber cognition or at previous stages will simply start mixing the liquids together haphazardly. Adolescents who have reached the Orange stage will first form a general picture of the fact that you have to try glass A with glass B, then A with C, then B with C and so on. They will try all the various combinations one at a time. The implication is huge: the person in Orange begins to imagine different possible worlds, to question existing dogmas and social contracts.

This worldview has profoundly transformed humanity in the last two centuries, bestowing upon us unprecedented levels of prosperity and life expectancy. The possibility to imagine "what if" has also freed us from the oppression of caste systems and religions and replaced feudal governance with the rule of law and democracy. This worldview dominates management thinking today; it is the (often unconscious) perspective that permeates what is taught in business schools across the world.

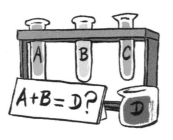

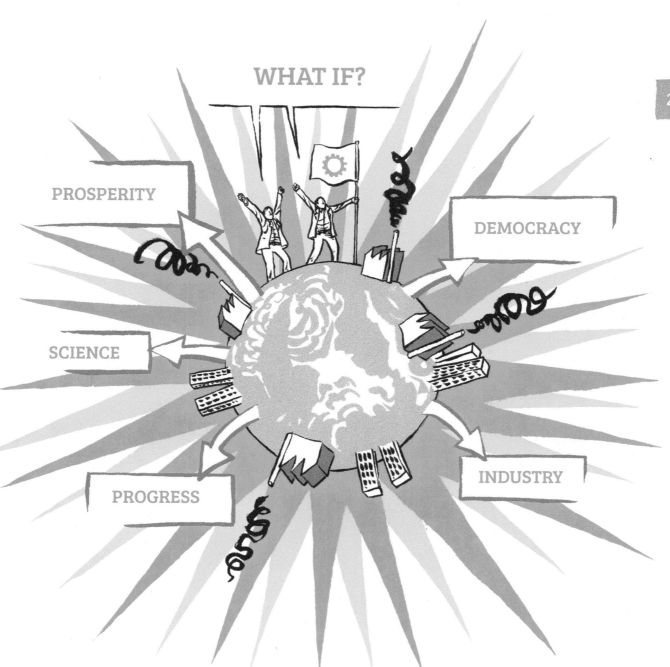

Orange Organizations?

Think publicly listed corporations, think Wall Street banks

The Achievement-Orange worldview profoundly shapes today's management practices. Most business leaders think along these lines, most MBA programs are based on Orange assumptions, most corporations rely on Orange management thinking. Take any global brand—Walmart, Nike, Coca-Cola, GE—and you are likely to find an Orange organization. Wall Street banks are perhaps the most striking examples: ruthlessly innovative and efficient machines in the pursuit of profits.

The dominant metaphor: organizations as machines

Achievement-Orange thinks of organizations as machines. The engineering jargon we use to talk about organizations reveals how deeply (albeit often unconsciously) we hold this metaphor. We talk about *units* and *layers*, *inputs* and *outputs*, *efficiency* and *effectiveness*, *pulling the lever* and *moving the needle*, *information flows* and *bottlenecks*, *re-engineering* and *downsizing*. Leaders and consultants *design* organizations; humans are *resources* that must be carefully aligned on the chart, rather like cogs in a machine; changes must be planned and mapped out in *blueprints*, then carefully *implemented* according to plan. If some of the machinery functions below the expected rhythm, it's probably time to inject some oil to grease the wheel with a "soft" intervention, like a team-building exercise. The metaphor of the machine reveals how much Orange organizations can brim with energy and motion, but also how lifeless and soulless they can come to feel.

Breakthrough 1: **Innovation**

Amber organizations rest on the assumption that the world is unchanging (or should be). With Orange comes the breakthrough of innovation: if you keep innovating and optimizing, and do so faster than the competition, profits and market share will come your way. This led Orange organizations to create departments such as R&D, marketing, and product management and to give birth to project teams and cross-functional initiatives—note how these are all absent in the Catholic Church or the public school systems, for instance.

Breakthrough 2: **Accountability**

To innovate more and faster than others, it becomes a competitive advantage to tap into the intelligence and creativity of many brains in the organization. The answer comes in the form of *management by objectives*. Top management defines an overall direction and cascades targets downward. People below are then given some freedom to find the best way to reach those targets.

A host of management practices was devised to support management by objectives, such as strategic planning, yearly budgets, key performance indicators, balanced scorecards, performance appraisals, bonus schemes, and stock options. Where Amber relied only on sticks, Orange came up with carrots and invented human resources in the process. (Again, notice how, for good or bad, these practices are almost absent, for instance, in public school systems or the Catholic Church—priests aren't assigned KPIs, as far as I know.)

Breakthrough 3: **Meritocracy**

From a historical perspective, meritocracy was a radical idea and a huge liberation. Not so long ago, it seemed natural that priests were recruited among the peasantry while bishops and cardinals came from noble families. The idea that a humble priest could become a pope wouldn't have occurred to anyone. Orange changed the narrative. In principle, anybody can move up the ladder. The smartest should lead the pack. The mailroom boy can become the CEO, even if that boy happens to be a girl or he has a minority background (in practice, of course, the playing field hasn't been entirely leveled). Resource planning, talent management, mentoring and coaching, leadership training, and succession planning are all Orange inventions. Job mobility is the norm; people are expected to change jobs every few years, and life employment is no longer seen as an ideal.

Orange's shadow

The scientific and industrial revolutions have brought us enormous freedom and prosperity. Increasingly, we also witness the massive shadow they cast on our future. One shadow is "innovation gone mad." With most of our basic needs taken care of, businesses increasingly try to create needs, feeding the illusion that more stuff we don't really need—more possessions, the latest fashions, a more youthful body—will make us happy and whole. We have reached a stage where we often pursue growth for growth's sake, a condition that in medical terminology is called cancer. It results in a predatory economy that is depleting the world's natural resources and killing off the very ecosystems upon which our survival depends.

Another shadow appears when success is measured solely in terms of money and recognition. When the only successful life is the one that reaches the top, we are bound to experience a sense of emptiness in our lives. The midlife crisis is an emblematic disease of life in Orange organizations: for twenty years, we played the game of success and ran the rat race. And now we realize we won't make it to the top, or that the top isn't all it's made out to be. When all boils down to targets and numbers, milestones, and deadlines and yet another change program and cross-functional initiative, some people can't help but wonder about the meaning of it all and yearn for something more. The Orange worldview is solidly materialistic—there is nothing beyond what we can touch—and our longing for meaning, for being in touch with something bigger than ourselves, has nowhere to turn.

GREEN (pluralistic) worldview

People at this stage[6] are keenly aware of Orange's shadows: the materialistic obsession, the social inequality, the loss of community, the harm inflicted to nature. They strive to belong, to foster close and harmonious bonds with everyone. They insist that all people are fundamentally of equal worth, that every voice be heard.

In the late eighteenth and nineteenth centuries, a small circle of people operating from Pluralistic-Green started championing the abolition of slavery, women's liberation, and freedom of religion. This worldview really came to the fore when it powered the counterculture of the '60s and '70s. Today, while Orange is predominant in business and politics, Green is very present in postmodern academic thinking, in nonprofits, and among social workers and community activists.

A new metaphor:
organizations as families

Leaders of Green organizations insist that people are more than cogs in the organizational machinery. Listen to these leaders, and it is striking how consistently they refer to their organization as a family, or a community, where everyone has a place, where colleagues look after one another, where the happiness of every member is important to the organization's overall success.

Breakthrough 1: **Empowerment**

People operating at this stage have a natural dislike for hierarchies. Green organizations therefore try to downplay hierarchy and to empower employees, to push decisions down to the lowest level. One image often used in Green organizations is the inverted pyramid: front-line employees are on top, and the senior executives and the CEO at the very bottom are servant leaders in service to the employees. Middle managers are trained to be coaches to their teams, to lead from behind and inspire, instead of directing from above.

Breakthrough 2: **Values-driven culture**

In Green organizations, shared values aren't simply a fig leaf hiding a basic pursuit of profit or market share. They truly inspire employees, they provide guidance to empowered employees to make the right decisions, and they often replace some of the thick books of rules and policies most organizations feel are needed to keep people in line. Getting the culture right is often the primary focus of CEOs in these organizations.

Breakthrough 3: **Stakeholder value**

Green organizations question the concept of "shareholder value," where a company's primary obligation is to maximize profits for shareholders. They insist that businesses have a responsibility not only to investors, but also to employees, customers, suppliers, local communities, society at large, and the environment and that they must balance all these interests.

Southwest Airlines, Ben & Jerry's ...

Green perspective on management can often be found in nonprofits, NGOs, and social ventures. But it is also found increasingly in the corporate world, where people have come to realize the importance of "soft" aspects of management. Green organizations often strive to inspire their employees to great things, leading them to outperform more traditional command-and-control organizations.[7] Southwest Airlines, Ben & Jerry's, and The Container Store are well-known examples of organizations whose founders have championed Green organizational practices.

The contradictions of Green organizations

There are some wonderfully vibrant values- and culture-driven organizations, so we know it works. And yet, making decentralization and empowerment work on a large scale is no easy feat! There is an inherent contradiction in the Green organizational model: it aspires to be egalitarian and consensus seeking, but it retains the hierarchical, pyramidal structure of Orange. There is often a disturbing disconnect between espoused values and reality, which causes disappointment and confusion. How do we make decisions here? Is it by consensus, or is it the boss who ultimately decides? In practice it's often a murky combination of the two.

In many smaller organizations, in particular in nonprofits or social ventures, the emphasis lies with consensus seeking. More often than not it leads to organizational paralysis. To get things moving again, unsavory power games break out in the shadows. Large, successful Green organizations seem to focus on empowerment more than strict consensus seeking. Deep down, they would love to function without the pyramid, without the need for bosses. But they haven't found a way to do it in practice. So they make do with a traditional, hierarchical structure but ask top and middle managers to give up some control and empower their subordinates. To most people, this doesn't come easily (especially when they are still responsible for delivering the numbers). Successful Green companies have found that they need to invest and keep investing a lot of time, energy, and money to train and remind managers to be empowering, servant leaders. Effectively, they aim to create a culture that is so vibrant and empowering that it more than compensates for the problems that inevitably come with the hierarchical structure.

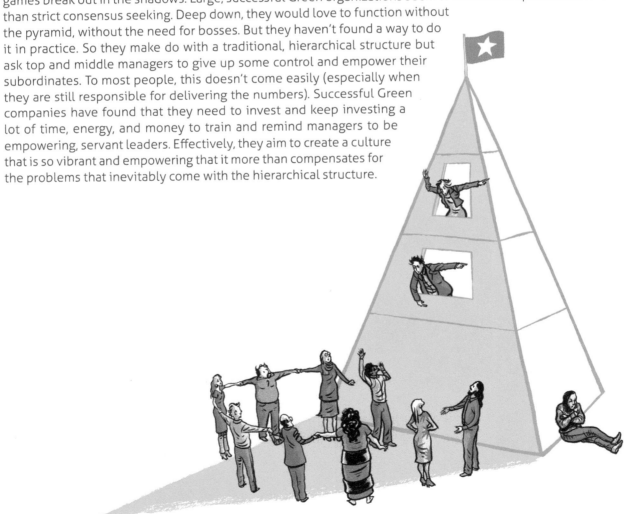

Hey, you! The whole stage thing sounds pretty insulting to me. Care to repeat it again?

Progress is only smoke and mirrors! We need to go back to rules and traditions.

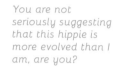

You are not seriously suggesting that this hippie is more evolved than I am, are you?

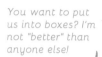

You want to put us into boxes? I'm not "better" than anyone else!

Let's clarify a few things.

Some people love frameworks, others not so much

Some people are ill at ease with the idea that people and organizations develop in stages. They don't like the idea that some people would somehow be "better" than others, more "evolved" than others. I very much understand the source of their concern. In the course of history, people have done much harm to one another in the name of some people being superior to others—take slavery, colonialism, racism, or sexism. And yet, there is no wishing away the huge evidence that humanity and human beings evolve, and do so in leaps. Here might be a more helpful way to think about it: people at later stages are not "better," but they can hold more complex perspectives.

A framework is a useful simplification.
But no organization is 100% "Orange" or "Green."

This developmental framework helps us make sense of different worldviews. And yet, let's be careful not to oversimplify! I cringe when I hear people say that someone "is" Amber or Orange. We know that things are far more complex. People can operate in one part of their lives from, say, an Orange perspective, and in others, from an Amber one.

So what do I mean when I talk about, for instance, an "Amber" organization? I refer to the organizational processes, structures, and culture, not to the people. An Amber organization is one where the majority (but not all! No organization is ever a pure breed) of the management practices are informed by Conformist-Amber thinking. In other words: the way the organization recruits, manages performance, makes budgets, sets targets, formulates strategy, etc., are mostly done in ways consistent with Conformist-Amber thinking.

Let's take an example: How do the different types of organizations handle compensation and incentives?

Sharing the spoils

In Red, the boss decides how to share the spoils, choosing to increase or reduce pay however he likes (think Mafia or drug lord). There are no formal processes for negotiating pay, nor any formal incentive processes.

Same work, same pay

In Amber organizations, salaries are typically fixed and determined by a person's level in the hierarchy (or other fixed status marker, such as the person's diploma or degree). There are no individual salary negotiations, no incentives.

Individual incentives

Orange believes strongly in individual targets and incentives. If people reach predetermined targets (that ideally are part of a budget or a cascaded system of targets), they deserve a sizable bonus. Large pay differences are deemed acceptable, if they reflect people's merits and contributions.

Team bonuses

Because the Green paradigm stresses cooperation over competition, individual incentives make way for team bonuses in Green organizations. Leaders aim to reduce excessive wage disparities that would undermine a sense of fairness and community (for instance, through a maximum multiple between the CEO's pay and the median pay).

Here is a summary of the four organizational models that exist today

IMPULSIVE

TRADITIONAL

ACHIEVEMENT

Division of labor

Replicable processes

Innovation

Accountability

Top-down authority

Stable organization chart

Meritocracy

What might the next one look like?

PLURALIST

EVOLUTIONARY

Empowerment

?

Values-driven culture

Stakeholder value

TEAL (evolutionary) worldview

A new stage of consciousness is currently coming to the fore that Ken Wilber gives the color Teal and that I sometimes call Evolutionary.[8] Because it is still very much emerging, it's too early to say how this will end up shaping the world. But quite a few scholars (Maslow, Graves, Kegan, and others) have studied how people who make the leap to Teal look at the world. And they report that, once more, it is a profoundly new worldview, one that opens radical new possibilities. So what are some markers of this worldview?

The world as a place for individual and collective unfolding

The world in Teal is no longer seen as fixed and God-given (Amber), nor, say, like an intricate, soulless mechanism (Orange). Instead, the world is seen as a place where we are called to discover and journey towards our true self, to unfold to our unique potential, to unlock our birthright gifts. This is like a Copernican revolution in an age that tells us we should strive to succeed, that we can become anything we want, if we only put our mind to it. People who embrace a Teal perspective learn to let go of pre-conceived ideas of what they should be and learn to listen within to go where life calls them.

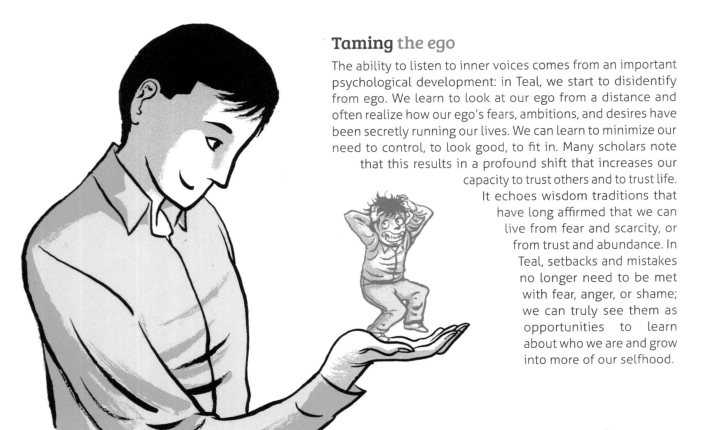

Taming the ego

The ability to listen to inner voices comes from an important psychological development: in Teal, we start to disidentify from ego. We learn to look at our ego from a distance and often realize how our ego's fears, ambitions, and desires have been secretly running our lives. We can learn to minimize our need to control, to look good, to fit in. Many scholars note that this results in a profound shift that increases our capacity to trust others and to trust life. It echoes wisdom traditions that have long affirmed that we can live from fear and scarcity, or from trust and abundance. In Teal, setbacks and mistakes no longer need to be met with fear, anger, or shame; we can truly see them as opportunities to learn about who we are and grow into more of our selfhood.

Inner rightness **as compass**

When we are fused with our ego, we are driven to make decisions informed by external factors—what others will think or what outcomes can be achieved. In Evolutionary-Teal, we shift from *external* to *internal* yardsticks in our decision-making. We are now concerned with the question of inner rightness: *Does this decision seem right? Am I being true to myself? Is this in line with who I sense I'm called to become? Am I being of service to the world?*

Yearning for wholeness

Many people who shift to a Teal perspective start to keenly sense the pain and emptiness in modern life, where we have separated from much of our true nature. We have let our busy egos trump the quiet voice of our soul; we are part of a culture that celebrates the mind and neglects the body; we so value the masculine that we neglect in us the feminine; we have lost community and our innate connection with nature. This realization often triggers a deep yearning for wholeness, for reuniting with all of who we are, with others around us and all forms of life and nature. It is not driven by a moral imperative (we should care for nature!) but by a deep realization that we are all deeply interconnected, deeply one.

What could this mean for organizations?

When people shift perspective in such profound ways, it is easy to speculate that they will structure and run organizations very differently. But really, there is no need to speculate. As we will discuss in the next part of the book, there are organizations out there that *already* operate along Teal principles and practices. And by now there are enough of them for us to have quite a good understanding of how Teal organizations can be structured and run.

PART 2

How do these new organizations work, then?

To make sense of something new, it's always good to start with a story

Here is the story of neighborhood nursing in the Netherlands and of a pioneering organization called Buurtzorg. Since at least the eighteenth century, every neighborhood in the Netherlands has had one or more nurses that worked outside of hospitals, visiting the sick and the elderly in their homes. During the twentieth century, the social security system increasingly took over the costs of the system.

In the 1980s, the Dutch government had an idea that made a lot of sense, seen from an "Orange" scientific/industrial perspective: if all the nurses could be grouped into large organizations, economies of scale would kick in, generating savings for the taxpayer. Nurses were pushed to affiliate with large organizations that started implementing modern (Orange) management practices step by step.

Quickly, these organizations decided it was inefficient that the client would always be seen by the same nurse. A different nurse was now dispatched to clients every day, based on availability. Higher flexibility meant less potential downtime for nurses between two clients. Call centers were set up in headquarters, now that clients could no longer call "their" nurse directly.

Then, it was decided to have the nurses specialize. More experienced nurses must be paid more, so they were sent to do only the more difficult, technical interventions. All the rest—simpler things like shots and bandages—was now pushed to less expensive nurses, resulting in further cost savings.

Step by step, the Orange machine logic took over

Managers noticed that some nurses worked much faster than others, so time norms were established. Two-and-a-half minutes to change a compression stocking, ten minutes for a shot. Everything was specified down to the minute. With time norms defined, planning departments were set up in headquarters. Every evening, each nurse now receives a sheet of paper with a detailed plan for the next day, prepared by someone in the planning department she most likely will never meet.

From 8:00 to 8:05, I'm expected at this address. I have five minutes to come in, say hi, change two compression stockings, and be out again.

The planner's program calculated that it will take me three minutes to drive to my next client …

… where I'll have ten minutes to give a shot …

And, predictably, these corporations started merging

The care providers started merging in pursuit of further economies of scale. To "manage" the nurses in these big companies, layers of hierarchy were added. A district manager overseeing a few dozen nurses reports to a regional manager, who reports to a national manager. The managers today often have no nursing experience. Their role is simply to monitor and improve the nurses' performance. They have lots of data they can slice and dice because nurses are asked to peg a small barcode sticker to the front door of all clients, scan that code when they go in to provide care, and scan it again when they leave. With all this data, managers can make continuous improvement; they can tell nurses for which kind of interventions they are slower than their peers.

Every one of these changes—specialization, flexibility, economies of scale, continuous improvement—has resulted in efficiency gains, arguably a good thing for the Dutch health care system.

But there is a dark side to the system

Patients hate it

For older, sometimes confused clients, having an unknown face come into the intimacy of their home every day is difficult. They have to share their story and their medical condition with a total—and hurried—stranger.

Nurses hate it

The way they are asked to operate hurts their vocation and integrity. They realize that they often give bad or insufficient care. But the system prevents them from doing what they know is called for.

A nurse named Jos de Blok created Buurtzorg in 2006 ...

Jos had been working as a nurse for ten years and experienced firsthand the changes forced onto his profession. Disgusted, he quit his job and created Buurtzorg. It would operate entirely differently. Quickly, he found that a self-organizing team of ten to twelve nurses with no manager and no team leader was perfect to provide great care—and a great work place.

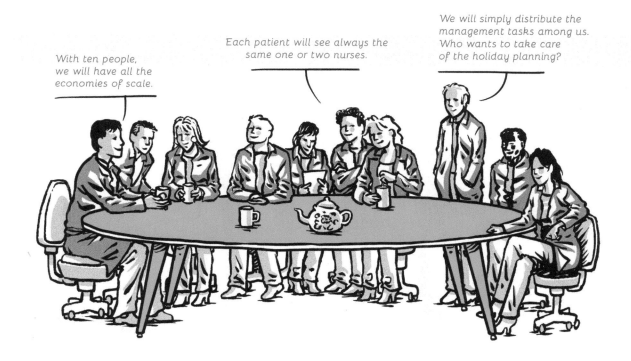

With a whole different perspective on health care

Care, at its best, is a small miracle that happens, or not, in the relationship of a patient and a nurse. That miracle never shows up when a mechanical perspective is applied to care. The best care will happen, de Blok is convinced, when nurses are seen as professionals, when they are trusted. Give them freedom, and they will offer truly great care.

The first thing a nurse from Buurtzorg does with a new patient is to sit down and drink coffee

Nurses often assist the patients in creating a network of support, to feel less alone and less dependent. For instance, they often help older patients and their children learn how to be there for one another during illness.

It's not unusual that nurses help their patients get to know neighbors to tie a network of support. The degree of care and intimacy between the nurses and the patients can be quite extraordinary. Often they journey together for years, sometimes until the very last moment, helping the patient depart in peace.

Buurtzorg has become
a spectacular success story

Patients and nurses love Buurtzorg so much that nurses have been deserting traditional nursing companies in droves. Every month, Buurtzorg receives hundreds of applications from nurses wanting to jump ship. Buurtzorg now employs more than nine thousand nurses, or two-thirds of all neighborhood nurses in the Netherlands! The nine thousand nurses all work in small teams of ten to twelve nurses, without a leader in the team and with no manager above them. No one times the nurses' interventions with patients. The whole nine thousand-strong company is managed with a headquarters of just twenty-eight people.

A few years ago, a study from Ernst & Young[9] found that Buurtzorg uses less than 40 percent of the hours prescribed by the doctor.

Because instead of just working off a crazy schedule, we now help patients become autonomous as much as possible

Thirty percent of all emergency hospital intakes are avoided.

We know the patients so well that we can detect problems early on.

Buurtzorg saves the Dutch social security system hundreds of millions of euros every year.

We have colleagues who are now trying to apply the same principles in psychiatric care, youth care, and other fields. And nurses from all over the world are setting up similar organizations in their countries.

Buurtzorg is just one of several extraordinary pioneers that are reinventing management

Buurtzorg

Home care nonprofit in the Netherlands, 9,000 employees

RHD

Human services nonprofit, United States, 4,000 employees

Sun Hydraulics

Manufacturing of hydraulic valves and manifolds, global, 900 employees, for profit

Heiligenfeld

Network of mental health hospitals, Germany, 600 employees, for profit

Morning Star

Tomato harvesting, transport, and processing, California, 400-2,400 employees, for profit

Holacracy

Organizational "operating system" adopted by many organizations throughout the world

FAVI

Brass foundry, automotive supplier, France, 500 employees, for profit

ESBZ

Publicly financed grade 7-13 school in Berlin, Germany, 1,500 teachers, students, and parents, nonprofit

Patagonia

Outdoor apparel maker and retailer, United States, 1,350 employees, for profit

AES

Global producer and distributor of electricity, 40,000 employees worldwide (2001), for profit

BSO/Origin

IT services, 10,000 employees worldwide (1996), for profit

Sounds True

Multimedia publishing company, United States, 90 employees and 20 dogs, for profit

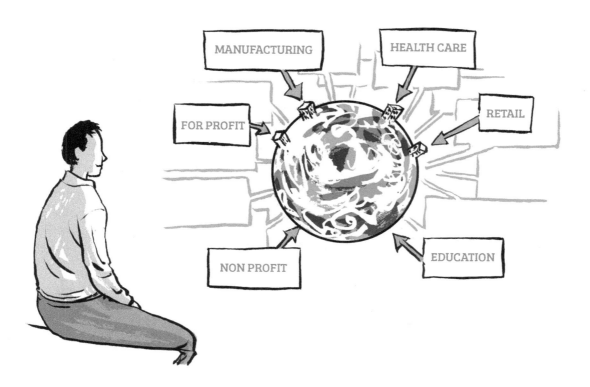

Many different industries, many different geographies ... but not your usual suspects

The previous page gives an overview of twelve organizations that I researched in depth and that already operate to a significant degree based on Teal principles and practices. They are not your usual suspects—these days we often read about management at Google, Apple, or Facebook. The organizations I researched don't have ping-pong tables or sushi bars, but their management practices are in a different league.

I find it quite remarkable that among these twelve organizations there are nonprofits as well as for profits, blue- and white-collar environments, and industries ranging from manufacturing, power generation, and food processing to health care and education. It seems that this new paradigm can operate in all sectors. It's also noteworthy that some organizations were founded with Teal ideas from the beginning, while others operated with traditional management practices before a new leadership transformed them.

I often get asked the question, "I wonder if this could work in my country?" Some of the companies I researched are based in Europe, others in the US, and some are truly global. I've come to believe that these management practices can operate in every type of culture because they tap into fundamental human needs, longings, and capabilities.

A new metaphor: organizations as living systems

Orange speaks of organizations as machines. Green uses the metaphor of families. Several of the founders of the Teal organizations researched for this book explicitly talk about the need for a new metaphor. Clearly, looking at organizations as machines feels soulless and clunky. People are more than cogs to be aligned on an organization chart. From a Teal perspective, the metaphor of the family can feel awkward too. Families, as we all know, can be mildly or wildly dysfunctional. And let's take the metaphor seriously: if I'm your boss and you are reporting to me, does it imply that I'm a father and you are a child?

The founders of Teal organizations use a different metaphor: with surprising frequency, they talk about their organization as a *living organism* or *living system*. Life, in all its evolutionary wisdom, manages ecosystems of unfathomable beauty, ever evolving toward more wholeness, complexity, and consciousness. Change in nature happens everywhere, all the time, in a self-organizing urge that comes from every cell and every organism, with no need for central command and control.

The metaphor opens up new horizons. Imagine what organizations would be like if we stopped designing them like soulless machines. What could organizations achieve, and what would work feel like, if we treated them like living beings, if we let them be fueled by the evolutionary power of life itself?

Teal organizations come with three breakthroughs that fundamentally challenge management as we know it

Self-management

Teal organizations have found the key to upgrading their structures from hierarchical, bureaucratic pyramids to powerful and fluid systems of distributed authority and collective intelligence.

Wholeness

Organizations have always been places that encourage people to show up with a narrow "professional" self. Teal organizations have developed a consistent set of practices that invite us to drop the mask, reclaim our inner wholeness, and bring all of who we are to work.

Evolutionary purpose

Teal organizations are seen as having a life and a sense of direction of their own. Instead of trying to predict and control the future, members of the organization are invited to listen and understand what the organization is drawn to become, where it naturally wants to go.

The three breakthroughs reinforce each other ...

... but companies don't necessarily have to embrace all three. Of the twelve organizations I researched, Buurtzorg is probably the most advanced across the board. On the other hand, a company like Morning Star, that we'll soon meet, has pushed and refined the breakthrough of self-management to an extraordinary degree but has given less thought to wholeness and evolutionary purpose. In many ways, this is good news: it makes the task less daunting for leaders inspired to transform their organizations. I hear from many companies and nonprofits that are currently making the transition, and they generally focus, at least at first, on the breakthrough that to colleagues feels the most important.

Breakthrough 1
Self-management

We thought we needed
hierarchy and pyramids

We now know how to create
much more powerful and fluid
systems of distributed authority

Get ready for this: at Buurtzorg with its 9,000 people, no one is the boss of anyone else

And it's not only Buurtzorg. Other large and very successful organizations operate entirely without the familiar pyramid, without managers. I know this might sound outrageous. Can it be true? We have a hard time wrapping our heads around this. I'll be honest: I wasn't expecting this when I started my research. I thought I would find "empowered" organizations with very few layers of management. But *no* layers of management? I thought that was impossible.

This is because I've grown up, like most of us, believing that it's possible, perhaps, for a team of four or five people to operate without a boss. But any group larger than that—at least I once thought—needs a structure, needs a boss, needs someone to call the shots! The truth, I now understand, is that large groups need structure and coordinating mechanisms, but can operate more powerfully without bosses! Our world is becoming too complex for us to continue operating with the pyramid we inherited a few thousand years ago.

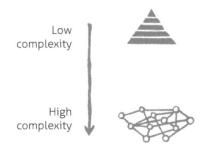

For a team to work well, you need to have a boss, someone to call the shots!

We've tried to get rid of bosses ... and frankly, it doesn't work.

Really?

Low complexity

High complexity

In environments where complexity is low, pyramidal structures with layers of hierarchy can work well. The few people at the top can make sense of all the complexity and make good decisions.

When complexity increases, the pyramid breaks down. The few people at the top, however smart they are, don't have enough bandwidth to grasp and deal with all the complexity.

Hierarchy cannot cope with complexity

It's almost become a rule today: CEOs and top leaders are hopelessly overworked. Any decision that requires some coordination, some broad perspective, has to pass by them, because in pyramidal organizations it's only at the top that reporting lines converge. They often feel uneasy, nervous about making decisions with only a few facts and arguments presented to them. But like workers on an assembly line, a decision must be made, one way or another, and it's off to the next decision ... or the company grinds to a halt.

Time at the top is so precious that people below often spend weeks preparing for a thirty-minute slot they are given with the executive committee. Many important decisions actually never get a slot, never get made. Other decisions made at the top turn out to be poor, even disastrous, because of politics or because people at the top simply don't have time to really understand what's going on in the field. In a complex world, the pyramid turns into a bottleneck. Even if people at the top throw in more hours, it's a structural problem that more hours won't solve. So what's the alternative?

The alternative, funnily enough, is all around us. All the complex systems that exist in the world—and there are many!—operate based on structures of distributed authority. Not a single complex system works with a pyramidal hierarchy, because such hierarchy always breaks down in the face of complexity.

The global economy?
Too complex for a central
planning committee!

The global economy is a hugely complex system—millions of companies, billions of consumers, making trillions of choices every day. It operates with structure and coordinating mechanisms, but there is no boss. The idea that we need a Soviet-style central planning committee to try to control the complexity has been completely discredited. And yet, we still cling to the idea that we need such central committees in organizations (where we call them the executive committee or the management team).

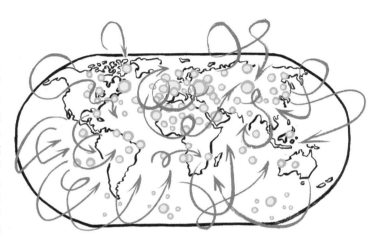

The human brain: 85 billion cells,
and no executive committee, no middle managers

Take another example: the brain we have in our head. It has 85 billion cells, and many more connections. There is a structure, there are coordinating mechanisms, but not bosses. Imagine one cell saying, "I'm the CEO. Any important thought has to pass by me for approval and by these six cells that I've chosen to be my executive committee." The brain is much too complex to be operated in a pyramidal fashion. It would stop functioning immediately if we tried.

Birds in a flock don't knock each other out

There can be hundreds of thousands of birds in a flock, flying at high speeds. And in the blink of an eye, when a predator appears, this whole dense cloud changes direction. How do the birds avoid mass collisions? It's almost a miracle. Hierarchy and centralized decision-making could never master this level of speed and complexity. Coordination is embedded in three rules that all birds play by.[10] Coordination mechanisms, rather than hierarchy, keep the flock agile and safe.

Take an ecosystem such as a forest
and imagine running it with layers of hierarchy

Let's take another example: a forest is a hugely complex system. There are billions of living beings ranging from microscopic organisms to massive trees. The whole system cooperates in extraordinary powerful ways. Let's imagine the winter sets in early. The whole ecosystem will adapt at once in a wonderfully complex interplay of the species. Now imagine trying to handle that with a traditional pyramidal structure. The largest tree—the CEO—would tell everyone to hold it until he and his buddy trees from the executive committee have come up with a plan. That plan, when it's ready, get's communicated in a cascaded way until the instructions reach the last worm, insect, and bacterium. But by that time, it's likely that spring will have set in!

Here is the good news: we now know how to operate large organizations without power hierarchy

Buurtzorg has more than nine thousand people today, and there are no managers, no bosses. Other organizations operate in similar ways. They have found ways to import the principles that fuel truly complex systems in nature into the workplace. We now know how this works. I've noticed that as soon as I talk about self-management, all sorts of misunderstandings arise. We often try to make sense of something new by projecting old thoughts onto it. So let's try to get some misunderstandings out of the way before we go any further.

Please! Self management can never work. In real life you need some structure!

If you like to spend your days in endless meetings, be my guest!

This is all still very experimental.

Misperception #1

Many people assume that self-management means that there is no structure, that everything is informal, chaotic. The mistaken assumption here is that "no bosses = anybody can do what they want." That's not the case. In self-management, just like in nature, there are structures and coordination mechanisms. People work in defined roles and there are processes for how to make decisions, how to deal with conflict, and so forth.

Misperception #2

The common assumption here is: "self-management = consensus decision making = endless meetings." Be reassured: that's not the case. Self-managing organizations work with decision-making mechanisms that are both simpler and more powerful than consensus. Actually, in self-managing organizations, there tend to be *many fewer meetings* than in today's workplaces.

Misperception #3

Another misconception: that self-management is still somehow experimental and unproven. The reality is that there are organizations out there, such as W. L. Gore, the maker of Gore-Tex; Morning Star, a tomato processing company; and others that have operated in self-managing fashion for decades. They have gone through economic booms and busts and have been shown to be remarkably resilient—like ecosystems. More resilient, in fact, than most traditional organizations.

Self-management requires that we upgrade almost all of the basic practices of management

Early attempts at self-management have often failed because people took a shortcut. They simply decreed: let's get rid of hierarchy and bosses. The company's backbone was ripped out without putting a new structure in place. The result: power vacuum and chaos. For self-management to work, it's not enough to take hierarchy out. We need to grow a system of distributed authority, which requires that we upgrade almost all existing management practices and structures.

This brings up lots of questions. *What structure should replace the pyramid? Who can make what decisions and how? Who decides who deserves a pay raise? Do we still need budgets and targets? Who gets to see what information?* These are very practical questions that need concrete answers. The good news is that there are enough successful self-managing organizations out there for us to know how each of these topics can be addressed. We pretty much have all the answers to these questions. Here is a list of the most important management structures and practices that need upgrading.

The next few pages illustrate a few of these practices

ORGANIZATIONAL STRUCTURE	BUDGETS
STAFF FUNCTIONS	TARGETS
INFORMATION FLOWS	PERFORMANCE MANAGEMENT
DECISION-MAKING	COMPENSATION AND INCENTIVES
MEETING ARCHITECTURE	CONFLICT MANAGEMENT
PROJECT MANAGEMENT	CRISIS MANAGEMENT
INVESTMENTS	DISMISSALS

Organizational structure

For the longest time, we thought
we needed a pyramid to organize human activity

Layers of hierarchy bring order and stability to large organizations. But everywhere around us we see signs that the pyramid finds it hard to cope with the complexity of the world today. We need to upgrade to structures of distributed authority.

So what's the structure of a place like Buurtzorg, then? The core unit is a self-managing team of ten to twelve nurses. Today there are eight hundred such teams throughout the Netherlands. In the teams, there is no team leader; the management tasks are spread out among the nurses. One person, for instance, deals with weekend planning, another takes the lead in recruitment, a third is the contact person with the local hospital, and so on.

Above the teams, there are no managers. For every forty to fifty teams in a region, there is a regional coach that teams can call when they need help to sort out a problem. The coach has no power over the team. Nor does she have any targets to reach or profit-and-loss responsibility. She is just there to help. Her role is significant nevertheless. Self-management is no walk in the park, and when teams get stuck, they are happy to be able to draw on the help of the coach.

And the headquarters? There are only twenty-eight people working in headquarters, mostly involved in administrative tasks such as interfacing with the Dutch social security system. They are truly "support functions"; they cannot impose procedures or guidelines from the top in the way staff functions usually do. Beyond that, there is no executive committee, no "head of" HR, finance, sales, or marketing that you would normally expect. The overall structure is really extraordinarily simple.

Teams of
self-managing
nurses

Support from
coaches and HQ

Here is another example:
an automotive supplier structured almost exactly like Buurtzorg

Self-management has proven itself in many industries. There are, for instance, a number of very successful factories that operate in this way. One of them is FAVI, a five hundred-person brass foundry in the north of France that produces gearbox forks for the automotive industry, among others. It was founded in the 1950s and was run for decades in traditional ways: there was a CEO, an executive committee (sales, HR, finance, engineering, maintenance ...), and in the factory, a *chef de production* commanding the *chefs de services*, who commanded the *chefs d'ateliers* who commanded the *chefs d'équipes* who commanded the workers!

Then in 1983, a new CEO was appointed: Jean-François Zobrist, a maverick and charismatic former paratrooper who turned FAVI upside down. Today, FAVI operates on lines very similar to Buurtzorg. There are thirteen self-managing "mini-factories." Most mini-factories serve a specific client: there is the Volvo team, the Volkswagen team, the Audi team ... and there are a few upstream production teams (the foundry team, the mold repair team) and support teams (the engineering team, the sales support team, etc.). Above the teams, there is no layer of management, no executive committee, other than the "CEO" (more on the role of the "CEO"— the quotation marks are deliberate—in Part 3 of this book).

FAVI's results are quite extraordinary. All its competitors have moved to China to enjoy cheaper labor costs, yet FAVI is not only the one producer left standing in Europe; it commands a 50 percent market share for its product. Its quality is legendary, and its on-time delivery close to mythical: not a single order has shipped late in over twenty-five years. FAVI's profit margins are so high that most years, despite Chinese competition, workers make sixteen or seventeen months of salary, thanks to profit sharing. There is virtually no employee turnover; workers who have tasted FAVI's ways of working can't see themselves going back to traditionally run factories.

65

How an order gets processed perhaps best illustrates how self-management transformed FAVI

This is how it used to work when FAVI was still run traditionally. A *sales manager* who received a client order instructed someone in *sales support* to enter the order into the system.

The *planning department* gave sales an estimated shipping date and allocated the necessary machine time in the *master planning*.

The day before production, the *scheduling department* made the *detailed planning* of what would be produced on which machine.

Based on the schedule, *HR* then allocated *workers* to machines.

Workers simply needed to show up and do what they were told. They had no idea if the order book was full or empty, or what client they were producing for.

This fragmented process was a black box, for sales account managers as much as for workers. If an order was late, it was hard to explain what had gone wrong.

Today the process at FAVI is much simpler

Once a week, the sales account person from, say, the Audi mini-factory meets with his teammates to share the order for the week. Everyone joins in the joy if the order is large or the disappointment if the order is small. Planning happens on the spot, and the team jointly agrees on a shipping date. Sometimes, the sales account person has bad news to share: Chinese competition quoted a very low price. Can we match it? People knock their heads together and figure out if they feel they can shave another few minutes off the machining process. The teammates don't have—and don't need—targets or bosses. They face their clients and competitors directly and know that their jobs depend on doing a good job and making wise decisions. They are proud of the work they do and their capacity to self-organize.

Decision-making

We've grown up believing there are basically three ways to make decisions.
Unfortunately, none of them works particularly well in organizations.

TOP-DOWN (HIERARCHICAL)   CONSENSUS   VOTE (MAJORITY RULE)

The advice process: the critical innovation underpinning self-management

I find this fascinating: several organizations independently discovered a better decision-making mechanism. One company called it the Advice Process, a name that captures its essence well.[11] The principle is that anyone can make any decision, including spending company money. But first, that person has to seek advice from 1) people who have expertise about the topic, and 2) from those that will be meaningfully affected, that will have to live with the decision.

The decision-maker must consider all advice seriously. But the goal is not to make a watered-down compromise. After careful consideration, the decision-maker chooses what he sees as the best course of action, even if that means going against a piece of advice received from a colleague.

In practice, the advice process proves remarkably powerful. Any person who feels strongly about an issue or a possibility has the power to do something about it. And at the same time, every decision is informed by a form of collective intelligence, as everyone who has something meaningful to contribute is heard.

Perhaps you wonder: does it really work? Do people really seek advice and listen? What prevents people from pretending to listen and then making a decision they had wanted all along? Here is why people take the advice process very seriously: they are on both ends of the equation all the time. Imagine that one morning, you give advice to a colleague. Of course, you hope that she will consider it very carefully. And so later that day, when the same colleague comes to you to give you advice on a different topic, it will be hard for you to simply dismiss her advice. Everyone is enmeshed in a deep network of advice-giving. In these workplaces, if you shoot from the hip, colleagues will quickly let you know that your behavior is unacceptable.

With the advice process, there is no need for hierarchy, no need to seek approval, to escalate decisions upwards. No need to try and get a topic on some committee's agenda, no need to play politics.

Let's take an example: a worker can decide to buy a new machine

When a new machine is needed, one of the machine operators can step up to lead the decision-making process. He can set up a list of specifications and negotiate with machine suppliers. Along the way, before he makes any decision, he must consult people with expertise and people who will be meaningfully affected.

None of my friends who work in other companies believe that I'm trusted to buy a machine that costs hundreds of thousands of dollars.

When I drew up the specs, I consulted Pete, the engineer who works in R&D, to find out if future products have specific machining requirements I need to take into account.

I sat down with Jayla from finance, who helped me review my calculations and gave me advice from a financial perspective. And Janet has a lot of expertise in negotiations. I learned a great deal there too.

And of course, at various points in time, I consulted my colleagues who will operate the machine with me. With all these perspectives, I feel I made the right decision. We are all pretty excited about the new machine! Back in the day, an engineer and a purchaser decided what machine to buy, and we would discover the machine only on the day it was installed. No wonder we dragged our feet to use it.

The bigger the decision, the more people need to be asked for advice

For small decisions related to your work, you simply go ahead and make the call. If the decision is somewhat more important, you might pop your head in a colleague's office or send out an email. Often, a team meeting might be a good place to get quick advice, if everyone on the team is concerned. For a larger decision—take the purchase of the machine, for example—you are likely to set up meetings along the way, ad hoc, when needed.

What about decisions that affect everyone in the organization? Well … everyone must be consulted! How is that possible in a large organization? Let's imagine that for some reason, the way overtime is calculated needs changing at Buurtzorg. That affects all nine thousand nurses. Jos de Blok has found a simple and powerful way to go about it. He seeks advice with a blog post. He writes posts regularly, often at ten o'clock at night, from his couch at home. He shares directions the company could take, decisions he feels are needed, or simply a story that epitomizes what Buurtzorg is about. The posts are written straight from the heart, without PR polish.

When he has a decision in mind that affects all the nurses, he shares his proposal and the thinking behind it and asks for reactions. The next day, the message is read by thousands of nurses when they log on between two clients. And it draws dozens, sometimes hundreds, of comments. And then one of two things happens. Most often, the comments signal that nurses agree with Jos's proposal. In the evening, twenty-four hours after the initial blog post,

Jos writes from his sofa again to confirm the decision. Sometimes, however, the comments show disagreement. Nurses share that from their perspective, things are more complex than Jos seems to realize. In such situations, when Jos is back on his sofa in the evening, he simply writes another message saying, in essence: "Oops, you are right. My proposal was premature." He then either makes an updated proposal, integrating the advice received. Or if things are really complex, he suggests creating a volunteer work group to look into the situation and come up with a solid proposal.

This kind of leadership by blog post requires a degree of trust, candor, and vulnerability that few CEOs in traditional companies would feel comfortable with. Once a post is published, there is no going back. Critical comments and rebukes are for all to see; they cannot be erased and can hardly be ignored. And where the discussion goes is beyond the CEO's control.

But consider the upside! I marvel at the efficiency of the process: a twenty-four-hour cycle to make decisions. Decisions that are already supported by the whole organization, to boot!

Contrast this with how a traditional organization may have decided about a change to the overtime formula.

The CEO would ask the head of HR to make a proposal.

The head of HR would task a junior member of the HR team with writing a draft.

A few days later, the two would meet to review the draft proposal. Most probably, the head of HR would have a few comments and they would meet a second, perhaps a third time.

The proposal is then discussed at an executive committee meeting. Maybe politics will come into play. Someone wants to look smart and insists on investigating some alternative option.

And the head of HR Is back to the drawing board with the junior team member.

Two weeks later, in the next executive committee meeting, the proposal is finally endorsed.

Now it goes to someone in internal communications who wordsmiths the document ...

... that the head of HR presents
in a meeting to all regional managers ...

... who in turn cascade it down in meetings with their nurses.

So MANY meetings! But that's how we tend to do things today. Perhaps you understand why I sometimes smile when people tell me: "But the advice process must take a lot of time!" In reality, it tends to be ruthlessly efficient. The quality of the decisions is often much higher too, because insightful perspectives have emerged and been integrated. Every decision is fueled by a process of collective intelligence. I wonder if you noticed: in the example where HR was tasked with making a proposal, no one ever consulted the nurses. It could well be that the decision proves unworkable on the ground. By the time people find out, it's too late and it will take another long and painful process to revise the decision.

Compensation and incentives

It doesn't need to be complicated

I find this slightly insulting, to be honest!

One of the first questions people often ask is: so when there are no more bosses, who gets to decide who makes how much money? Who gets a pay raise or a fat bonus?

Talking about bonuses, here is an interesting finding: none of the organizations I researched believes in individual or team incentives. For instance, at FAVI, no one is incentivized, not even the sales people. Actually, sales people at FAVI don't even have targets. I write this, and I realize that by now I might have lost some of you: sales people without targets and the promise of a fat bonus, seriously? But come to think of it, a sales person at FAVI, say from the Audi or the Volvo team, meets his colleagues every week to tell them about the weekly order. He sees how everyone cheers when the order is large and how there is disappointment when the order is small. His teammates' livelihood depends on a healthy order book. What more incentive does he need? From a Teal perspective, it's almost insulting to believe that someone will work hard just because you dangle a carrot in front of their face. If a person isn't motivated to do great work, something is up. Let's talk about the issue and try to discover what blocks the person's inner motivation. But today, in many workplaces, we simply accept that most people aren't motivated, and we try to buy them off with the promise of a fat bonus (despite the fact that research shows that bonuses don't work or are even counterproductive).[12]

Instead of bonuses, many organizations I researched simply share a part of the profit with everyone when profits are abundant. I've mentioned how at FAVI, for instance, in most years, machine operators will make the equivalent of fifteen or sixteen months of salary, thanks to the company's profit-sharing scheme.

But what about the base pay? Who gets to decide who deserves a raise, for instance? The most elegant process I've seen comes from a company called Morning Star in California.

Morning Star is the company in this research that has fleshed out, perhaps better than any other, the processes required for effective self-management. It was started quite humbly in 1970 by a man named Chris Rufer, who leased a truck to haul tomatoes. Today Rufer heads a small tomato empire: Morning Star harvests tomatoes, runs a two hundred-truck hauling business, and has become the world's largest tomato-processing company. It operates three state-of-the-art processing plants that produce 30 to 40 percent of the tomato paste and diced tomatoes consumed in the United States. Chances are that if you've been to the United States and you're not allergic to spaghetti sauce, ketchup, or pizza, you've enjoyed Morning Star's products more often than you know. The company is in a commodity industry, and yet it is highly profitable. Chris Rufer has been able to finance the growth mostly from cash flows and remains 100 percent owner of his business. Morning Star came up with a number of technical innovations, but self-management can certainly be credited for much of its success.

At Morning Star, pay increases are self-initiated. If you work there, once a year, you write a letter in which you state what raise you think you deserve. You also discuss with colleagues in your area who wants to volunteer for this year's salary panel that will provide advice.

People are remarkably good at estimating their value. In any given year at Morning Star, roughly three-quarters of colleagues will go simply with a cost-of-living increase and a quarter with a salary raise on top of it. Sometimes the salary panel tells colleagues they've been too humble—it really happens. And in a handful of cases, the panel tells people they might have aimed too high. In such cases, the panel has no authority to force the colleague to accept its advice. But if a colleague seems to be really unreasonable, the panel can invoke an extra step: a conflict resolution mechanism that creates the space to find a solution agreeable to everyone.

The remarkable thing about the advice process is that it cuts through much of the strategizing, haggling, and complaining about compensation. You think your salary is too low? Simply make the proposal to raise it and see what happens. At Morning Star, salary is not something people waste much time talking about. Like many other practices, the way self-managing organizations deal with pay forces us to grow up, to behave as adults. Boss–subordinate relationships often push us to behave like parents and children, where subordinates rebel and complain and bosses get annoyed at the perceived immaturity of the people they manage.

Performance management
What prevents people from simply slacking off?

It's hard to find motivated people these days.

You just have to have managers to keep the pressure up!

In traditional organizations, it's the leadership's role to put pressure on the system, to challenge subordinates to do more and do things faster. When that pressure disappears, will people not simply start to slack off?

Many self-managing organizations have found the opposite, as strange as it might sound. At Buurtzorg, for instance, nurses need to help one another set healthy boundaries and not work *too much*. What is happening here? How come people without bosses don't become complacent? The short answer seems to be this: *intrinsic motivation*, calibrated by *peer emulation* and *market demands*.

Most workplaces slowly but surely sap people's motivation. Young recruits often beam with energy and with ideas. But then, again and again, their ideas get lost in the quicksand of the company's decision-making. At the same time, they are regularly asked to comply with some absurd decisions made high up the pyramid. At some point, they settle for less and say, "Simply tell me what you want, and I'll do it." When people cannot express their talents, something in them dies a little. But this can be reversed: nurses who join Buurtzorg often share that they feel like they've somehow found new life. All of us are happier at the end of a day where we did great work rather than lousy work. When nothing stands in the way of our intrinsic motivation, we tend to be … well, motivated!

Peer emulation plays a big role too. At Buurtzorg, teams see every month how they compare with others in terms of productive hours.[13] This information is public. When a team lands at the bottom of the list, antibodies (or call it pride) kick in: there will always be a team member who will call a team meeting to discuss the situation. The same is true when one team member isn't pulling her weight: at some point, another team member will raise the issue. You can hide from a boss. It's much harder to hide from colleagues.

And then there is market demand. Remember how changes at FAVI brought workers in much closer contact with their clients? Every week, workers know about the order their mini-factory receives. Workers have full transparency and know that if they drop the ball, Chinese competitors would love to pick it up. Reality is a more powerful motivator than hierarchy.

No power hierarchy = lots of natural hierarchies!

One last word about self-management to put aside another frequent misunderstanding. It's true that in self-managing organizations, there is no more power hierarchy: there is no boss who has the power to hire and fire you, to determine your pay raise, or to decide if your idea should be implemented. But this doesn't mean that everyone is equal. Quite the opposite—in the absence of a *power* hierarchy, lots of *natural, healthy* hierarchies start to emerge.

Let's take Buurtzorg as an example. Whatever the topic, some nurses will naturally have a larger contribution to make or more say, based on their expertise, interest, or willingness to step in. One nurse might be a particularly good listener and coach to her colleagues. Another might be a great planner and organizer. Another might be a living encyclopedia of arcane medical conditions. Yet another might have a knack for handling conflict within the team or within the feuding family of a patient. Some nurses build up reputations and influence well beyond their team and are consulted by nurses from across the country in their area of expertise. Because there is no team manager, space becomes available for other natural and spontaneous hierarchies to spring up—fluid hierarchies of recognition, influence, and skill.

This is not about making everyone equal. Some people will tend to focus on narrower roles, say a machine operator focusing on the work related to a certain set of machines. And others will contribute with a broader perspective, say an engineer that takes the lead in designing a whole new factory. But the engineer has no power authority *over* the operator, not on hiring, firing, or salary. The genius of mechanisms like the advice process is to channel decisions and resources fluidly to the most appropriate person: sometimes the engineer will ask the operator for advice, and sometimes it will be the other way around. The goal is not to make everyone *equally*

powerful, but to make everyone *fully* powerful. This is best understood using a metaphor from nature. A fern or a mushroom growing next to a tree might not reach as high as the tree, but that is not the point. Through a complex collaboration involving exchanges of nutrients, moisture, and shade, the mushroom, fern, and tree don't compete as much as they cooperate to grow into the biggest and healthiest versions of themselves.

It's the same in Teal organizations: the point is not to make everyone equal; it is to allow all employees to grow into the strongest, healthiest versions of themselves.

Breakthrough 2
Striving for wholeness

Enormous energy is set free when we finally drop the mask, when we dare to be fully ourselves

Wholeness in the workplace

For some reason, there are subtle pressures in organizations that push almost everyone to wear a professional mask. In a nearly literal sense we see this in the bishop's robe, the executive's suit, the doctor's white coat, and the uniforms at a store or restaurant. The uniform signals a person's professional identity and rank. It is also a claim the organization makes on the person: while you wear this uniform, you don't fully belong to yourself. You are to behave and show up not as you are, but in certain pre-determined, acceptable ways.

What is at play here is a subtle, but powerful, conspiracy of fears. Organizations fear that if people were to bring all of themselves to work—their moods, quirks, and weekend clothes—things would quickly turn into a mess. Armies have long known that people who are made to feel interchangeable are much easier to control. Employees, for their part, fear that if they were to show up with all of who they are, they might expose their selfhood to criticism and ridicule, that what they show might be used against them at some point. Many of us figure it's better to play it safe and to hide our selfhood behind a professional mask, to shut out part of who we are when we dress for work in the morning.

When I speak about this in public, sometimes people tell me, "I'm not sure what you're talking about. I'm the same at work as I am at home." I congratulate them, because in my experience, this is quite rare. But I also tell them that I believe that some of us have been wearing our masks for so long that we have forgotten that we wear it! We no longer know how to take it off, even at home.

Let me try to illustrate this. We all have an ego, a part of us that seeks success and recognition, that wants to look good, to win arguments in a meeting, and so forth. And we all have a deeper part, some deeper longings, deeper hopes for our lives, for other people, and for the planet. Strangely enough, in most organizations, we learn quickly that showing up from the ego is acceptable. It's the norm, in meetings, for people to battle for their point of view, for their career, or for their team's budget. But show up from a deeper place, and it won't be long before you feel exposed.

DEEPER SELF

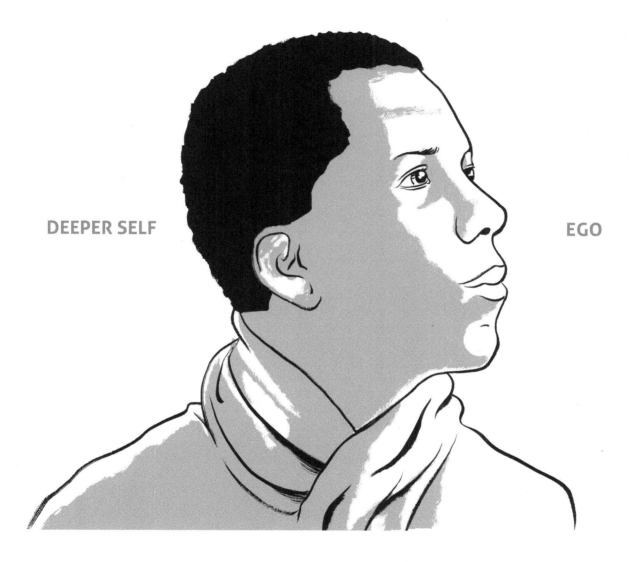

EGO

Speaking our truth feels risky

Imagine the following story. A creative young person is hired straight out of school by an advertising agency. (If you work in a bank, a hospital, or a school, feel free to adapt the story.) After working there for a year, he invites all his colleagues to an internal meeting. He tells them, *"Please show up. This is really important to me."*

At the meeting, he thanks them for being there and says, *"I've been thinking a lot lately. I wonder: what are we doing? I've come to see that we mostly create false needs, telling people they will be happy and whole only if they buy a product they don't really need. To create that false need, we tell them they are not OK the way they are, that they should look like the photoshopped, impossibly perfect women and men from our ads. All this to sell a product made in China, that uses up natural resources and pollutes the planet. And that will end up in a landfill a few weeks or months later. I really wonder: is this what we are meant to do with our lives?"*

That would be a courageous conversation to initiate! But I suspect this young person wouldn't have a long career with that advertising firm. Speaking our truth, giving voice to our deepest hopes and longings feels risky ... because in many work places, it *is* risky. And so we don't speak our truth. Worse: it's not just that we don't talk about it—I believe we often put a lid on our inner voice; we silence it even to ourselves. If, in so many work places, we play petty ego games, I don't believe it is because we are somehow fundamentally flawed as a species. Simply, the ego is what we are left with when we cut ourselves off from deeper parts of ourselves.

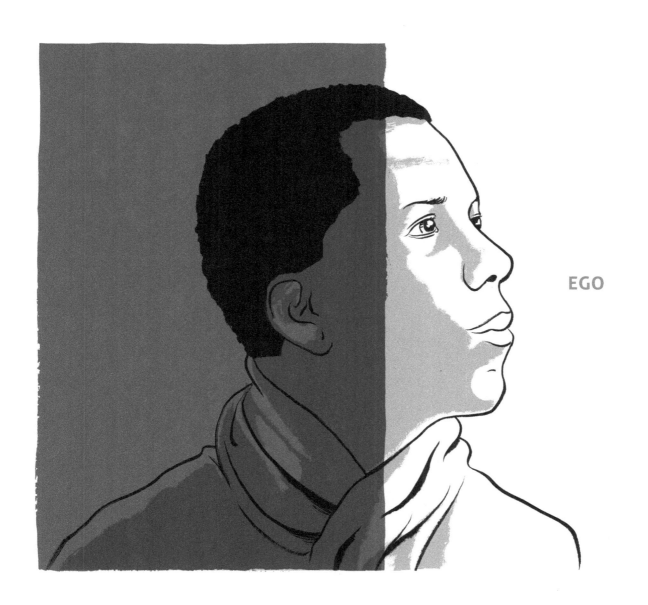

EGO

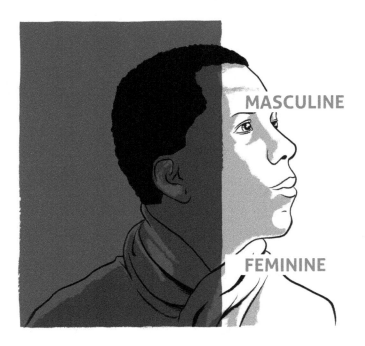

Let's take another dichotomy to explore this further. We all have masculine and feminine energies, whether we are male or female. In most organizations today, it doesn't take long to learn that showing up with our masculine energy is valued. It's good to appear determined, to have answers, to be actively building the future. And it doesn't take long for us to realize, albeit unconsciously, that showing up with our feminine energy (again, whether we are a man or a woman) is not a career winner: taking care of one another, being reflective, slowing down, sharing vulnerability—these traits won't get you in line for the next promotion. Often they are met with ridicule. And so we all end up appearing much more determined than we really are, hiding our doubts and vulnerabilities, losing touch with an essential part of who we are.

MASCULINE

87

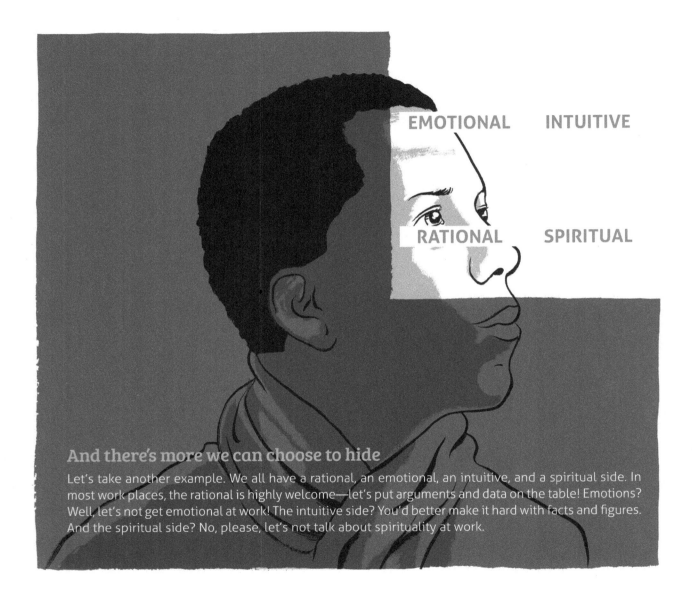

EMOTIONAL   INTUITIVE

RATIONAL   SPIRITUAL

And there's more we can choose to hide

Let's take another example. We all have a rational, an emotional, an intuitive, and a spiritual side. In most work places, the rational is highly welcome—let's put arguments and data on the table! Emotions? Well, let's not get emotional at work! The intuitive side? You'd better make it hard with facts and figures. And the spiritual side? No, please, let's not talk about spirituality at work.

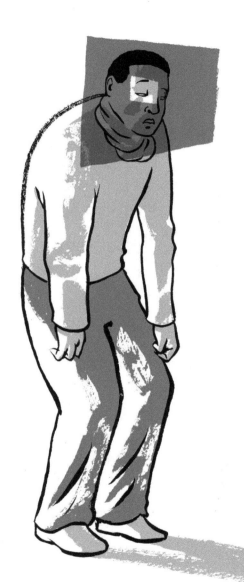

Work as a place
to strive for wholeness

In the illustration on the previous page, the person shows up with only one-sixteenth of himself. Of course this is only an illustration, but I think it speaks to a profound truth. If so many workplaces feel lifeless, it is perhaps because we bring so little life to work.

Self-management goes a long way toward reducing the many subtle fears people experience in the workplace. When there is no boss to please, no people below to keep in line, much of the poison in the organization gets drained. Some organizations, like Morning Star or FAVI, focus their efforts squarely on self-management. Other organizations find that even with self-management in place, being in community is not easy. We all have our personal histories, and in the presence of others, we often shy away from being fully ourselves.

For that reason, some organizations have put in place very deliberate practices that help us feel safe enough to be ourselves. In fact, it goes further than this: they found that work can be a wonderful place to discover parts of ourselves we didn't even know existed. The friction of working with others brings up wonderful possibilities to reclaim aspects of who we are that we have neglected or pushed into the shadows.

What happens then is magical. There is a level of vibrancy and aliveness in some of these work places that I had not seen before. Colleagues discover in awe how much more life there is in them than they ever imagined. Work becomes a vehicle where colleagues help each other reveal their inner greatness and manifest their calling. Much of what makes the workplace unpleasant and inefficient simply vanishes.

There is a sentence I heard over and over again from people working in Teal organizations: "Here I can be myself."

There is another extraordinary sentence I heard from people in three different organizations. "You know, sometimes I wish home was more like work." (!) They meant that there is a degree of listening and care among colleagues that they don't always have with their spouse or children.

It doesn't need to be difficult

Most of the practices that invite us into wholeness are surprisingly simple. And yet, we have grown so used to narrow, almost aseptic workplaces that your first reaction to what I'll share in the next pages might cause surprise or even unease: is this really appropriate in a work context? Take the following practice of Sounds True, a Colorado-based company that disseminates teachings of spiritual masters through audio and video recordings, books, and online seminars.

In the early days, Tami Simon, the founder and CEO of Sounds True, brought her dog along to the office. When the business expanded, it didn't take long for some of the colleagues she hired to ask if they too could bring their dogs to work. Today it is not rare for a meeting to take place with two or three dogs lying at people's feet (currently the company has twenty dogs along with its ninety employees). Something special happens in the presence of dogs, colleagues noticed. Petting a dog tends to ground us, to bring out the better sides of our nature. And when it's a colleague's dog we pet, or a colleague that pets ours, we subtly build community. The decision to open the company's doors didn't just let in dogs, but more life in general.

A similar thing has happened at Patagonia, the outdoor apparel maker. At its headquarters in Ventura, California, the company hosts a Child Development Center for employees' children, from the tender age of a few months up to kindergarten age. You can often hear children's laughter and chatter at the office, coming from the playground outside, from children visiting their parents' desks, or from kids joining parents and their colleagues for lunch at the cafeteria. It is not uncommon to see a mother nursing her child during a meeting. Relationships change subtly but profoundly when people see each other not only as colleagues, but also as people capable of the profound love and care young children inspire.[14] When colleagues have just played with a baby over lunch, it's that much harder to fly at each other's throats when they sit in a meeting.

Allowing dogs or children into the workplace is not earth-shattering. And yet it's highly unusual. Some people will argue that children or animals distract us from work. I have come to believe there is a deeper reason why we might feel unsure about it: we have found safety in hiding behind a professional mask at work. Animals and children uncannily get us to reveal a deeply loving and caring part of us. And in the presence of colleagues, frankly, that can feel vulnerable. But just imagine if not only you, but all your colleagues, were showing up in loving and caring ways? How much more would we all enjoy work? How would our relationships, our lives, be changed?

Existing practices need to be reinvented, and new ones added, to help us invite one another into wholeness

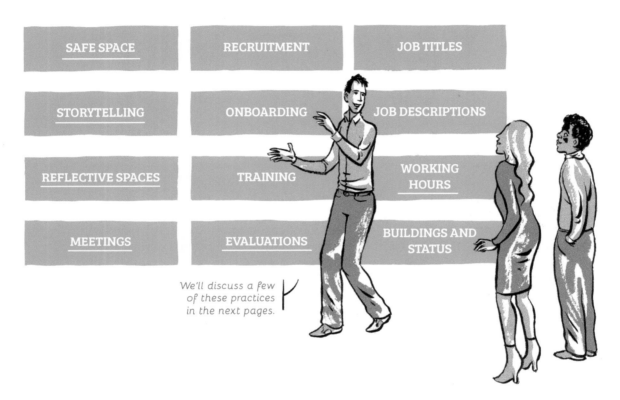

SAFE SPACE

RECRUITMENT

JOB TITLES

STORYTELLING

ONBOARDING

JOB DESCRIPTIONS

REFLECTIVE SPACES

TRAINING

WORKING HOURS

MEETINGS

EVALUATIONS

BUILDINGS AND STATUS

We'll discuss a few of these practices in the next pages.

Recruitment, onboarding, evaluations ... these fundamental HR processes can be reinvented in fundamental ways. Take recruitment: that's often where the lying starts. As a candidate we try to look the part, hiding everything that isn't gold. And so does the organization (a whole field called "employer branding" has emerged that tries to put a positive spin on how wonderful a workplace candidates might join). And so both sides start by trying to see through the other's pretense.

Could we invent a truthful, soulful recruitment process, where candidates and employer drop the mask and come from a place of wholeness?

Companies that invite the whole self to work, I found in my research, reinvent not only their HR practices. They also put in place some specific, foundational practices that we don't really have in today's organizations, such as creating safe space, inviting storytelling, or creating reflective spaces.

Safe space

Showing up whole feels exhilarating ... and vulnerable. It needs a space that feels safe.

All spiritual and wisdom traditions speak to the fact that we can live from two places: from fear and separation, or from love and wholeness. Our deepest calling in life, these traditions tell us, is to overcome fear and recognize the oneness beyond everything, to reclaim wholeness, within ourselves and with the world. Why then is wholeness so hard to achieve and separation so easy to fall into? Showing up whole feels risky. We put our selfhood out for all to see and expose this most treasured part of ourselves to potential criticism, ridicule, or rejection. Organizations that are serious about wholeness have found that the primary task is to create a safe space—a space where we feel safe enough to share with others our deepest gifts, doubts, and longings.

Resources for Human Development (RHD), a Philadelphia-based nonprofit, is an organization that has strived, for more than forty years, to do just that: create and maintain safe and open workplaces. It was started in 1970 with a $50,000 contract to provide community mental health services in suburban Philadelphia. Today, its 4,600 staff provide services worth $200 million to tens of thousands of people in need through programs in fourteen states that operate homes and shelters for the mentally ill, developmentally disabled, drug and alcohol addicted, criminally adjudicated, and homeless.

In ways not unlike Buurtzorg or FAVI, each of RHD's programs is run by a self-managing team with an average of twenty people. These units are responsible for their entire operation, from defining a strategy to recruiting and purchasing, from budgeting to monitoring results. Self-management is fundamental to RHD's extraordinary levels of care. But another ingredient is just as important: the safe and open environment RHD has managed to create in the units and throughout the company. RHD's purpose is to give care, day in, day out, to people who have experienced difficult, sometimes horrendous, journeys in life. In RHD's programs, in the homes and shelters, verbal or physical violence can flare up quickly. It would be easy for RHD's employees to see these people as broken, to fall into a pattern of "us" and "them." RHD has purposefully built up a culture and practices that help employees stay connected, from a place of deep humanity, with their colleagues and clients.

Beyond values, ground rules to create a safe environment

Creating safe workplaces starts with raising everybody's awareness that our words and actions can create or undermine a safe working environment. Unfortunately, we aren't taught this in school. Some organizations, like RHD, find this so critical that they capture in a document a number of ground rules that everyone should respect. At RHD, the document is called "Bill of Rights and Responsibilities for Employees and Consumers." It's a beautiful document that spells out what kind of behaviors colleagues wish to see, and what behaviors are deemed unacceptable. For instance, it discusses how to deal with conflict gracefully and speaks to five unacceptable expressions of hostility. To give you a sense of the document, the first unacceptable behavior—demeaning speech and behavior—is described in the following terms:

> *"Demeaning speech and behavior involves any verbal or nonverbal behavior that someone experiences as undermining of that person's self-esteem and implies that he/she is less than worthy as a human being. Such behaviors include, but are not limited to, name-calling, ridicule, sarcasm, or other actions which 'put down' people. Demeaning a person with such physical behaviors as rolling one's eyes when the person speaks or otherwise negating her importance as a member of the community is also unacceptable. Anyone encountering such hostile behavior has the right and responsibility to surface it as an issue."*

Green organizations have pioneered values-based cultures that, in one form or another, often include values such as integrity, respect, or openness. The detailed ground rules in Teal organizations essentially take shared values to the next level. Of course, it takes more than a document to bring values and ground rules to life. Many organizations in this research have chosen to start right at the beginning: all new recruits are invited, as part of the onboarding process, to reflect upon the values and ground rules in order to create a common language and common references across the organization. Other opportunities, like all-hands meetings, value days, or annual surveys, can be used to reconnect with and reaffirm the ground rules.

COMMON REFERENCE

Reflective spaces

We need reflective spaces for deeper truths to emerge

Wisdom traditions from all parts of the world insist on the need for regular silence and reflection to quiet the mind, if we are to let truth emerge from deeper places within ourselves. An increasing number of people take up and integrate a contemplative practice—meditation, yoga, walking in nature—into their daily lives. Many organizations researched for this book have set up a quiet room somewhere in the office, and others organize meditation and yoga classes. These practices open up space for individual reflection and mindfulness in the middle of busy days. Some organizations go a step further: they also create *collective* moments for self-reflection, which prove to be immensely powerful in building a culture of wholeness and a sense of community.

Heiligenfeld is the organization I know that has woven reflective practices most profoundly into everyday life at work. It is a fast-growing company with more than eight hundred employees running four mental health and rehabilitation hospitals in the center of Germany. It is the brainchild of Dr. Joachim Galuska, a medical doctor and psychotherapist. In the 1980s, he felt that more holistic approaches to therapy were needed to treat patients in mental hospitals; he wanted to add spiritual and transpersonal approaches to classical psychotherapy. He found that none of the existing hospitals he talked to were open to his vision.

In 1990, he stumbled upon Fritz Lang, an entrepreneur and owner of a historic, if somewhat faded, hotel in a small spa town. Together they decided to transform the hotel into a small forty-three-bed mental health hospital that would offer a holistic approach to therapy. The success has been remarkable, with clients traveling in from all over Germany and other parts of Europe, pushing Heiligenfeld to keep expanding and to post solid financial returns.

A whole set of reflective practices

At Heiligenfeld, it is considered normal—even essential—that there be moments for employees to pause, to reflect, to share struggles with colleagues and learn from them. A whole set of practices ensures that space for this is created within life's normal business:

- The company offers every new employee the opportunity to learn to meditate. And every day, there is a thirty-minute meditation session planned for anyone interested.
- Every employee—cleaning staff, cooks, and everyone else—who struggles with an issue can book individual coaching sessions from a surprisingly vast menu of coaching techniques.
- All work teams pause somewhere between two to four times a year to work with an external coach through any tensions or upsets.
- More unusual: four times a year, Heiligenfeld organizes a "mindfulness day"—a day that patients and staff spend in silence (staff whispers when needed). It's a day that many employees look forward to. Collaborating in silence brings a special quality to relationships; it requires being mindful in new ways, listening—in the absence of words—to the presence, emotions, and intentions of one's colleagues.

The practice that probably does most to invite reflection and foster a sense of wholeness and community happens every Tuesday morning. For seventy-five minutes, 350 colleagues (ideally it would be everyone, but some colleagues need to be with patients[15]) come together to pause and engage in joint reflection. There is a new topic every week, which can range widely: colleagues have reflected on conflict resolution, dealing with failure, company values, interpersonal communication, bureaucracy, IT innovations, personal health, and more.

The meeting always kicks off with a short plenary presentation to frame the subject matter. Let's say the topic is "dealing with failure." The presentation briefly introduces ways to deal gracefully with failure.

My way of dealing with failure, frankly, is to freeze. I want to pretend that nothing happened, hoping it will just go away …

After this introduction, people shuffle their chairs around to create groups of six to ten people. This is the heart of the Tuesday meeting: in the confines of these groups, colleagues reflect on the topic—how they deal with failure in their lives, at work, and at home, individually and collectively. Every group elects a facilitator who enforces a few ground rules to create a space where it's safe to explore, to be authentic and vulnerable.

At some point, a microphone goes around the room and people who feel inclined to do so share what came up for them in the discussion. There is no expected end product; everyone comes out of the meeting with his or her own personal learning. And yet, collective insights and ideas often surface, and important initiatives regularly emerge from these conversations.

I had a pretty cool insight this morning. I realize that I'm really tired of always trying to be so perfect in everything I do! I've come to see that …

These large-group reflections are a time-consuming practice, for sure—seventy-five minutes every week for more half of the company. But ask people at Heiligenfeld, and they tell you the benefits far outweigh the costs. The large-group reflections are like a company-wide training program on steroids; the whole organization grows its way through one topic after another, week after week.[16] The common experience also fosters community and a common language beyond what can be achieved by any other practice I know of. Every week, the ground rules of how people relate with one another get reaffirmed. The trust, empathy, and compassion that get nurtured there end up permeating the whole organization. To approving chuckles in the room, an employee of Heiligenfeld stood up at the end of one of these Tuesday meetings and said, "You know, I wish I could have more Heiligenfeld at home, too!"

Storytelling

Reclaiming the power of stories

In self-managing organizations as well as hierarchical ones, trust is the secret sauce of productive and joyful collaboration. But it's hard for trust to flourish when everyone is hiding, to some degree, behind a professional mask. We don't just lose productivity; in subtle but real ways, our humanity feels cheated by the shallow relationships we have when we don't engage with each other at levels that truly matter. If we want workplaces of trust, if we hope for deep, rich, and meaningful relationships, we have to reveal more of who we are. Going bowling together can be a fun break from work, but such "team building" activities are generally more of the same: they keep to the surface and don't really foster trust or community at any deep level. These events lack the essential element we have used to build community and create shared narratives since the dawn of time: the practice of storytelling.

Sharing stories can be woven into life at work in many ways. The Center for Courage & Renewal, a small nonprofit that helps teachers and other leaders "rejoin role and soul," has a beautiful practice when it recruits a new staff member, for instance. Team members welcome the new recruit in a special gathering where each shares a wish for him or her, and they tell the story of their wish with an object that symbolizes it. It's a thoughtful way to make the newcomer feel welcome. But in many ways, it serves existing team members just as much, as they too get to know one another at a deeper level. Each wish, each object is a story that reveals what the storyteller cherishes about the workplace and about their colleagues.

When teenagers step into their power

ESBZ is a grade 7-13 school in Berlin, Germany, that is extraordinary on many counts. Students self-manage their learning to a large degree. Teachers self-manage too (the school is structured in "mini-schools" of three classes and six teachers), and so do the parents who contribute three hours per month to the school in self-managing teams. Students and teachers credit one practice as particularly defining for the school's extraordinary spirit of learning, collaboration, and maturity: the "praise" meeting (which is entirely prepared and run by students). Every Friday afternoon, the school's big hall is packed with three hundred children, teachers, and administrators.

They start by singing a song together, to settle into community.

And then it's open mic. Anyone—student, teacher, or staff—can walk up to the microphone ... and praise or thank someone.

I want to thank Hanna.

On Tuesday, I was really down. It really helped me when you told me ...

And so it continues for half an hour of praise and gratitude.

After the praise comes a moment for constructive criticism ("Speak your mind"), and the gathering generally wraps up with announcements, celebrations, and prayers.

Every praise is essentially a miniature story that reveals something about two people—the storyteller and the person being praised or thanked—in their struggles and in their glories. Think about how extraordinary this is! Teenagers tend to wear not one, but many, masks because what their peers think matters so much to them. It speaks volumes about ESBZ that students find the courage to stand up and praise others publicly, that they find it natural, every Friday, to share stories that are funny, touching, and heartfelt in front of hundreds of their peers! It is part of the human condition that everyone at some point feels down, confused, or stuck, and at others grateful and overflowing with joy. I wish students (and adults!) everywhere could experience what it means to be heard and respected in such a way, that they could experience the sense of community when this happens.

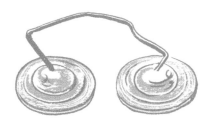

Meetings

Our egos love meetings.
One more reason to reinvent how we do them.

Self-managing organizations tend to have many fewer meetings. But regardless: meetings are places where our egos often feel like they need to make a strong appearance. In front of a group of people, we fear looking stupid or weak. We don't like to lose an argument or to make a proposal that meets with embarrassed silence. And yet meetings can also bring out the best in human nature. They can be places of true collaboration, where everyone contributes from their strengths, where we can speak to what we truly care about. Almost all organizations researched for this book have instituted specific meeting practices to help participants keep their egos in check and bring more wholeness to the conversation.

Some methods are quite elaborate. Buurtzorg, for instance, uses a decision-making process consisting of several steps that prevent ego-hijacks and keep conversations focused. (It bears striking resemblance to a process called "Integrative Decision Making" in Holacracy, a self-managing framework that is gaining traction throughout the world). Other methods are very simple. At Sounds True, every meeting starts with a minute of silence. FAVI, for many years, had the practice of starting every meeting with all participants sharing a brief story of someone they had recently thanked or congratulated. The practice creates a mood of possibility, gratitude, celebration, and trust in other people's goodness and talents. It helps to shift the focus away from self-centered goals and toward reconnecting with the broader needs of the organization. At Heiligenfeld, a pair of palm-sized cymbals called tingsha bells lies in every meeting room. Every meeting starts with the question: who is going to ring the bells today?

I'm happy to do it this time.

I participate in the meeting like everyone else. But I have an added role: whenever I feel the discussion comes from ego or turns somewhat unsafe ...

... I ring the bells.

The rule of the game is that no one can speak until the last sound of the cymbals has died out—which takes a surprisingly long time! During that time, everyone reflects in silence: what is happening right now?

Almost always, that's all it takes to get the meeting back on track.

Colleagues at Heiligenfeld are now so used to this practice that the bells rarely sing. People told me that in many cases, it's enough for a person to simply reach for the bells for someone to say, "Okay, you're right, I'm sorry." I still find this amazing: of course everyone in the company still has an ego, but people learn to tame it. Imagine—meetings without egos. I sometimes chuckle when I remember the executive committee meetings in traditional corporations I've been invited to join over the years. Had they used this practice, the only sound you'd have ever heard would be the singing of the tingsha bells!

Commitment and working hours

Let's honor all the important commitments in our lives

We live in corporate cultures that ask us to pretend that work is the overriding commitment in our lives. I know few managers who would dare to cancel an important meeting for their child's school play. Or because a good friend needs help. Or simply because the wind today is beyond perfect for surfing, and there might not be another day in the year like this. The few that do cancel a meeting to attend their child's play often feel they need to invoke some false, but more acceptable, pretext. The cultures in many workplaces ask us to disown some of the very things we care most about.

In workplaces that honor wholeness, we can stop pretending that work trumps everything else. We can have honest conversations about all the important facets in our lives. What a relief to be seen in the fullness of who we are and to discover how rich our colleagues' lives are with commitments of all sorts.

The structure of small, self-managing teams helps in providing flexibility when someone needs to change his or her working routine for something important, at short notice. Nurses at Buurtzorg can temporarily take on a few extra clients. An operator at FAVI can try to swap shifts by having a discussion with colleagues. This happened in a mini-factory when a man was building a house. To be onsite with the builders during the day, he talked to colleagues from the night shift: would someone be willing to swap shifts for a four-month period? An arrangement was quickly made—his request didn't need to go through an HR process or receive managerial approval.

In a self-managing setting, you can change your working hours when you need to. But you are expected to find a solution to uphold the commitments you have made. This expectation is the flip side of having no centralized HR function. You can't simply file a request with HR and then let them worry about solving the issue. In practice, colleagues tend to go out of their way to help you. They know that in turn, you might chip in when they need flexibility. It results in a culture of mutual support, where everyone accepts the simple truth that we have many commitments we want to honor in our lives.

See ya, the big boss called again, urgent stuff!!

On Wednesday night? We all know he's just picking his son up from a soccer game.

Performance evaluations

Performance evaluations don't need to be dispiriting affairs

Annual appraisal meetings are often the most awkward moments of the year. Employees, who often have received no feedback during the year, are nervous because they don't know what to expect. Managers are just as uneasy at the prospect of a personal, perhaps difficult, conversation and often stick rigidly to some assessment grid handed out by HR. Some managers, luckily, put their heart into this, and in some organizations, they even get trained in assessing employees. And yet, because much is tied directly or indirectly to performance evaluations—bonuses, raises, projects, promotions—the appraisal discussion is one tinged with fear. The goal is to establish a dispassionate, objective snapshot of one's performance. Everyone watches his or her words carefully, and the conversation rarely is spontaneous, rarely comes from the heart. No wonder people fail so often to be inspired by these conversations!

What would happen if we tried to hold these discussions not from a place of fear, but a place of deep connection, inquiry, and celebration? Into what's going really well. And into places where someone's knowledge, experience, talent, or attitude falls short, at least for now, of what the roles require. Beyond the current roles, two colleagues can inquire into even deeper questions: *What do I truly long to do? What is my offer to the world? What are some of my unique gifts? What holds me back? What could help me step more boldly into the life that wants to be lived through me?*

Sounds True has been experimenting with ways to turn the appraisal process into moments of true inquiry and celebration. In a first step, every employee reflects on his or her own performance and aspirations, based on a list of thought-provoking questions. The second step is the most unusual and beautiful. People who work closely together convene as a group. Live and unscripted, they offer everyone in the group, one person at a time, feedback and ideas to further nourish and stimulate their self-reflection. Say it's your turn. You take the seat of the feedback receiver. It starts with your colleagues settling into a minute of silence, closing their eyes and trying to hold you in their heart.

They aim to let go of any form of judgment to be able to offer feedback from a place of love and connection. In turn, every colleague takes the seat in front of you and shares two gifts with you. The gifts are their answers to the questions: *What is the one thing I most value about working with you?* and *What is one area where I sense you could change and grow?*

A note-taker transcribes the answers on a large piece of paper that he hands over to you, like a gift, when the round is done. The experience at Sounds True is that people feel held very lovingly in the process, and it's not unusual that tears well in gratitude of being seen and appreciated so deeply.

All the input received from colleagues helps employees to push and deepen their thinking in a third step, a one-on-one conversation with a colleague. (At Sounds True, which still has a hierarchical structure, this colleague is your manager, but in a self-managing structure, it could take place with a trusted peer.) *What do you take away from the discussions? What did you learn? What do you want to pay attention to in the future? Where do you feel called to go?*

I find this example extraordinary. Annual appraisals don't need to be dispiriting and lifeless. With the right presence and the right questions, we can turn them into rituals of celebration and deep inquiry into our selfhood and calling.

Breakthrough 3
Evolutionary purpose

What if we stop trying
to force the future into existence?

What if instead we simply dance
with what wants to emerge?

There is a reason
we are pretty cynical about
most "mission statements"

It has become standard practice, in almost all organizations, to formulate a mission statement that provides employees with inspiration and guidance. And yet, we've come to feel that most of them ring hollow because in practice they don't drive behavior or decisions. Executives, at least in my experience, don't pause in a heated debate to turn to the company's mission statement for guidance, asking, *What does our purpose require us to do?*

So if the collective purpose isn't what drives decision-making, what does? Almost always, it is the self-preservation of the organization. The fear-based nature of the ego in Red, Amber, Orange, and even Green predisposes leaders and employees to see the world as a dangerous place with competitors everywhere trying to steal their lunch. The only way to ensure survival is to seize every opportunity to make more profit and to gain market share before competitors do. In the heat of the battle, who has time to think about purpose? Sadly, this fixation on competition plays out even in organizations that are somewhat shielded from competition—say, in the military, public schools, and government agencies: the fearful ego still seeks safety, but this time in internal battles. Managers fight for the self-preservation of their units in turf wars with other units to secure more resources or get more recognition.

With the transition to Evolutionary-Teal, people learn to tame the fears of their egos. This process makes room for exploring deeper questions of meaning and purpose, both individually and collectively: *What is my calling? What is truly worth achieving?*

113

Does your organization have a noble purpose? Watch out! The implications might be radical

What happens when an organization *truly* takes its purpose seriously? Buurtzorg provides an interesting example. Remember: Buurtzorg uses the same syringes and bandages as other companies in home care; their only competitive advantage is their management philosophy and their organizational practices.

If Buurtzorg were to think like everyone else, they would try to make this their big secret, like Coca-Cola with its formula!

Instead, here is what Jos de Blok did: he wrote a book explaining Buurtzorg's method in great detail. And then he sent a copy to all his competitors.

His goal is for patients to live rich and autonomous lives. Whether Buurtzorg ends up with 20, 50, or 80 percent market share is not that important.

Jos accepts all invitations from competitors to give a talk—many of them want to understand how Buurtzorg attracts all their nurses and clients!

Two competitors are adopting Buurtzorg's methods, and Jos and a colleague have been doing consulting work for them. So far, they have never asked to be paid. Imagine this: a CEO actively coaching a direct competitor for free!

At some point in my research, I noticed something striking: I had almost never heard the word "competition" mentioned. Orange organizations are obsessed with competition, but here the very notion of competition seems to have vanished. Where has it gone? The answer, I came to see, is surprisingly straightforward: when an organization truly has a noble purpose, there is no competition. Anybody who can help to achieve the purpose on a wider scale or more quickly is a friend, an ally, not a competitor. That's how Jos de Blok and Buurtzorg look at the world.

The notion of evolutionary purpose stands for more than a noble purpose, though

It means that the organization *listens* and *dances* with that purpose (the term "evolutionary purpose" was coined, to my knowledge, by Brian Robertson, the founder and champion of Holacracy, an elaborate self-management methodology). Today's management is predicated on the desire to *predict and control* the future. A whole arsenal of practices supporting predict-and-control is now considered essential to any well-run firm (increasingly, this is asked also of nonprofits, schools, hospitals, and government agencies): strategic planning, mid-term planning, yearly budget cycles, KPIs, balanced scorecards, "SMART" targets, incentive schemes, and so forth. This fits the metaphor of the organization as a machine: a machine needs to have a boss who programs the machine, who tells it what to do. The CEO's role is to analyze what's happening in the world to devise a winning strategy for the future. And then he must ensure a proper execution of that strategy. Or, to take another metaphor that's often used, that of the sailboat: someone—the captain—needs to chart the course and then ensure that the crew sets the sails in the right direction. When I started this research, this is how I saw things too: Strategy – Execution. How else could it be?

Founders and "CEOs" of organizations like Buurtzorg, FAVI, or RHD no longer believe in predict-and-control.

They tend to see the organization not as a machine, but as a living organism that has its own energy, its own sense of direction, its own purpose to manifest in the world. The role of leaders—of everyone really—becomes much simpler. Rather than trying to predict and force a future into existence, they simply can listen to where the organization naturally wants to go … and then help the organization get there. When we do this, we always sail with the wind at our back. We go from *predict-and-control* to something much more powerful: *sense-and-respond*. Brian Robertson uses an insightful analogy to explain the shift.

Imagine if we rode a bicycle like we try to manage our companies today. It would look something like this.

We'd have our big committee meeting, where we all plan how to best steer the bicycle. We'd fearfully look at the road up ahead, trying to predict exactly where the bicycle is going to be when.

We'd make our plans, we'd have our project managers, we'd have our Gantt charts, we'd put in place our controls to make sure this all goes according to plan.

Then we get on the bicycle, we close our eyes, we hold the handle bar rigidly at the angle we calculated up front and we try to steer according to plan.

And if the bicycle falls over somewhere along the way ...

... well, first: who is to blame? Let's find them and get them out of here.

And then: we know what to do differently next time. We need more upfront prediction. We need more controls to make sure things go according to plan.

That's not how we ride a bicycle! When we ride, we constantly sense and respond. We are present, and with all our senses fully in play, we take in lots of input, consciously or unconsciously, and we continuously adjust to the reality in front of us.

It's not directionless: we still have a purpose pulling us forward. It's by being present to that purpose in every moment, not just once up front, that we are more likely to reach it.

If we are mindful as we ride, we might well discover a shorter way. Or a more beautiful one! Or perhaps we'll even discover a whole new destination that serves our purpose better.

The deep challenge here is that it requires letting go of our comforting illusion of control, the illusion that we've done our job as leaders: we've done all the analysis, we've got the plan, things are going to go according to plan. Paradoxically, it's only when we give up the illusion of control that we get the real thing, by shifting to sense-and-respond.

At FAVI, they use another metaphor to illustrate the switch from predict-and-control to sense-and-respond. "Traditional companies," they say, "look five years ahead and plan for the next year. We try to operate like farmers: we look twenty years ahead and plan for the next day." This new perspective is already deeply integrated in some project management techniques like Agile programming. Evolutionary purpose scales this to the whole organization. This has profound implications for all sorts of management processes. In many cases, the processes are radically simplified, and sometimes, they are no longer needed at all.

Strategy

No strategic planning?
You must be joking!

None of the twelve organizations I researched (all of which are remarkably successful) has a strategic document, a strategic plan for the next three or five years. That sounds crazy! Every business school tells us that strategy is the alpha and the omega of success. But then again, think about it: wouldn't it be much more powerful if an organization constantly listened to new opportunities and adapted accordingly, instead of doing a big strategic exercise every few years and sticking to the plan in the meantime?

So how does an organization continuously iterate on its strategy? There are a number of processes it can use. The simplest one is: do nothing special. Let self-management work its magic. There is a new vocabulary that often comes up with Teal pioneers: sensing. With self-management, everybody can be a sensor and initiate changes—just as in a living organism every cell senses its environment and can alert the organism to the need for change. We human beings are remarkable sensors. It's only that in traditional organizations, most of this sensing is filtered out because only the signals that make it to the very top (after being sometimes heavily distorted) are acted upon.

The simplest way to do sense-and-respond? Let it happen ...

Here's a story that illustrates this well. Buurtzorg, remember, gives care to people in their homes. At some point, though, Buurtzorg also began to work in the field of accident prevention. That was quite an addition to its strategy. How did Buurtzorg go about it?

It all began when a Buurtzorg team found itself pondering the fact that elderly people, when they fall, often break their hips. Hip replacements are routine surgery, but patients don't always recover the same autonomy. Buurtzorg should really do something in terms of prevention, they concluded. Two nurses got creative. They put in place a partnership with a local physiotherapist and an occupational therapist. They organized an evening presentation in the neighborhood to teach older people about how they could minimize the risk of falling down. And they took the occupational therapist to visit their clients in their homes, advised patients on small changes in habits, and discussed adaptation to their home interiors to avoid the risk of falling. They were very pleased with the program and talked to Jos de Blok. *As part of its purpose, Buurtzorg should really be doing prevention work*, they said. *This should be a company-wide program!* Now, if de Blok were a traditional CEO, this is what he probably would have done.

He would have created a task force to analyze the opportunity and make a recommendation.

From your analysis, it's pretty clear we should go for it.

Based on the recommendation, he would then make a choice: yes, we go for it, or no, we don't. If the answer were yes, he would have put aside a budget for the project and someone would devise a roll-out plan.

Let's start with a pilot region, and then every two months, another region goes live.

Jos de Blok's answer was quite different. Much humbler, you could say. Intuitively, the idea of doing prevention work made lots of sense to him. But who was he to know if this was really the right thing to do? So he made a simple suggestion to the team.

Why don't you write a short and catchy story about what you've done and publish it on our internal social network? Let's see how it resonates with other teams. And if you can, package your approach so other teams can quickly copy it.

Many other teams thought this was brilliant, and it wasn't too long before half the teams became, as it's now called, a Buurtzorg+ team (Buurtzorg + prevention). Here is the fascinating thing: no one person formally made the decision for Buurtzorg to go into prevention. The organization's own energy moved it in this direction.

This is how nature has worked for millions of years. Innovation doesn't happen centrally, according to plan, but at the edges, all the time, when some organism senses a change in the environment and experiments to find a response. Some attempts fail to catch on; others rapidly spread to all corners of the ecosystem. Reality is the ultimate referee.

But surely, some people have a greater sense of where to go?

This question goes back to a common misunderstanding—the goal is not to give everyone the exact same power. It is to make everyone powerful. So Jos de Blok, Buurtzorg's founder, can sense what he feels is needed, just like any nurse, and initiate a new course. The founders of many of the organizations I researched are visionary people, and they often are deeply attuned to what their organization might be called to do. And they can use the advice process to make it happen, just like everyone else.

More structured ways to listen

In self-managing organizations, a lot of the listening to purpose happens simply through people sensing what's needed and using the advice process to make it happen. More structured ways to listen can be baked into daily life, though. Some organizations use a very simple technique: in every meeting, people make sure there is an empty chair that represents the organization and its purpose. Anybody participating in the meeting can, at any time, change seats to listen to the organization and become its voice. Here are some questions one might tune into while sitting in that chair.

Sounds True has built a variation of the empty chair into a wonderful New Year's ritual they have. At the end of the ritual, colleagues sit together in silence and listen in: what does Sounds True ask from them in the year to come? Whoever wants to can then share with the group what came up for them.

Practices like the empty chair are really simple. There are also more elaborate practices that allow large groups of people to sense together where the organization wants to go. Otto Scharmer's Theory U, for instance, helps groups to let go of preconceived notions and let deeper insights emerge. Other methods such as Appreciative Inquiry, Open Space, Future Search, and World Café have proven their worth in helping very large groups of people—sometimes thousands of colleagues!—collectively unearth a direction for their organization's future.

Should we ban strategic thinking then?

Some organizations I've researched have never done a big strategic exercise. Sensing and responding on a daily basis does its magic. But it would be stupid to go overboard and say it should *never* be done. Sometimes a sudden change in the outside world requires a profound reflection about the future, leading to some big strategic decisions. The organization should simply resist casting the outcome in stone, feeling that its work of sensing is done for the next few years. Whatever strategy it chooses is just the basis that will evolve as of the next day, as people sense and respond, as in Buurtzorg's example.

What about the need for alignment, for shared priorities?

In many cases, the organization's purpose provides enough alignment. In Buurtzorg's case, all the nurses share the purpose of helping patients live rich and autonomous lives. But some organizations might find it useful to provide some more precise guidelines for the foreseeable future. HolacracyOne, the training and consulting organization behind Holacracy, a codified self-management system, has an elegant practice that revolves around polarities. Once a year, all the colleagues come together for a strategy workshop. In a first step, they try to build a collective sense of what's happening inside and outside the organization, resulting in stimulating discussions and walls full of Post-its. Based on this step, they then try to distill guidelines for the foreseeable future, which they express through simple polarities. For instance, there is a natural tension in HolacracyOne's business between innovation and standardization, and so one year people in the workshop decided that "for the foreseeable future, we prioritize *Documenting & Aligning to Standards* over *Developing & Co-Creating Novelty*." This is not an absolute rule; of course, the organization will not stop innovating. But it gives everyone a clear guideline that for now the emphasis is on standardization.

Budgets

How about budgets? Are those still needed?

Many traditional organizations go through a painful budgeting cycle every year, where they make revenue, cost, and profit predictions for the next twelve months. Front-line managers try to keep the numbers as low as possible, since they know that every month they will be asked to justify any shortfall. And top managers want them as high as possible, to keep the pressure on. Often, after tedious back and forth, some numbers are agreed upon that no one really trusts. The whole exercise is pretty meaningless anyway, when you come to think of it: for some reason, in a few months time, business will turn out to be much easier or much more difficult than expected, and so who can really tell if a manager that delivers 5 percent below or above targets has done a good or a bad job?

These processes are mostly meaningless and dispiriting. A more insidious consequence is that they fix our attention on making the numbers and distract us from sensing what's needed and possible. If budgets are so problematic, are they still needed in a world of sense-and-respond? Many organizations I researched don't make any budgets. Others do very simple budgets, when an important decision needs some prediction of the future.[17] Say your company wants to cover raw material contracts in advance: then of course, you need to make your best estimate of the volumes you think you'll purchase. In this case, all the units are asked to submit the numbers that are added up, and that is the budget. Once the decision is made, everyone forgets about the budget: budgets are not used to monitor performance. Organizations drop the painful discussions where managers are called in to justify why they didn't make the numbers. FAVI has a provocative internal mantra to explain their perspective on budgets: *our goal is to be profitable not knowing how, instead of losing money knowing exactly why.*

But then, don't people have targets? Well, no! None of the twelve organizations I researched has any form of top-down targets. (In some organizations, like Morning Star, people set their own targets, like a jogger might do to spur himself on.) Think of it: if you work in an organization where you have the power to make things happen, where you can bring all of who you are to work, where you serve some noble purpose, do you really need a carrot to do good work? If someone isn't motivated, the problem is not an absence of targets. Something is causing that work not to be stimulating for that person. That is the problem that needs fixing. Simply adding targets won't do it.

Change management

What happened to change management?

Earlier in this chapter, we discussed how Teal pioneers never talk about competition. Here are two other terms I didn't encounter even once during the research: *change* and *change management*. It's quite extraordinary! In traditional organizations, change is one of the most perplexing questions. It's discussed endlessly in management literature. A whole industry of experts and consultants in change management thrives on the idea that change is hard and often fails. In the pioneer organizations I researched, change seems to happen naturally and continuously. It doesn't seem to require any attention, effort, or management. What is going on?

In the machine paradigm, organizations are viewed as inanimate, static systems—a collection of boxes that stack up in a pyramid structure. Static systems don't have an inner capacity for change. Force must be applied to the system from the outside. Change in that worldview is not a fluid, emerging phenomenon, but a one-time movement from point A to point B, from one static state to another. Change in this worldview is an unfortunate necessity that we try to minimize by predicting and controlling the future. We seek to plan the surprises out of life. We pray that reality stays within the boundaries of the budget and the strategic plan. When it doesn't, we need change and a change program. We need to redesign the organization like we redesign a machine, moving people around to fit the new blueprint. Unfortunately, people resist being moved around. To overcome resistance, organizations often feel compelled to play on fears, telling frightening stories of how a hostile, competitive world threatens their survival if nothing changes. And how everything will be all right once we reach point B.

Living systems have an innate capacity to change

In a world where organizations are self-managing, living systems, we don't need to impose change from the outside. Living systems have the innate capacity to sense changes in their environment and to adapt from within. In a forest, there is no master tree that plans and dictates change when rain fails to fall. The whole ecosystem reacts creatively, in the moment. Teal organizations deal with change in a similar way. People are free to act on what they sense is needed; they are not boxed in by static job descriptions, reporting lines, and functional units. They can react creatively to life's emerging, surprising, nonlinear unfolding. Change is a given. It happens naturally, everywhere, all the time, mostly without pain and effort.

Mostly without pain and effort? I'm not meaning to sound naïve. At an individual level, when life calls for change, we always feel a tension, sometimes pleasant, sometimes unsettling. There are habits we have grown fond of; our identity is invested in certain situations. But when change isn't imposed from the outside, from above; when we personally feel the pull of change, the need for change; when we feel powerful and responsible; when there is a safe space where we can have meaningful conversations about all of this ... chances are that embracing change is somewhat easier.

129

Practices to upgrade to listen to evolutionary purpose

We have discussed how some practices—strategy, budgets, targets, change management—can be upgraded to go from predict-and-control to sense-and-respond. Other management practices are involved in this shift as well, including how we define which products are worth developing, how we go about marketing, and what suppliers we work with.

STRATEGY	MARKETING	BUDGETING & CONTROLLING
TARGETS	PRODUCT DEVELOPMENT	MOOD MANAGEMENT
COMPETITION	SUPPLIER MANAGEMENT	CHANGE MANAGEMENT

Page 160 lists a number of resources, including a wiki that spells out every one of the processes mentioned in this book!

Of the three breakthroughs, the notion that organizations have an Evolutionary Purpose, and that we can listen to that purpose, is perhaps the most subtle and far reaching. I notice that some people simply reduce this notion to the fact that organizations should pursue a meaningful purpose. I hope I've managed to convey that it is a much deeper change.

Of the three breakthroughs, I also think it is the one we still have the most to learn about. There is a lot of knowledge out there on how to invite wholeness. Even for self-management, we now have a solid sense of the practices involved. When it comes to listening to purpose, while we have a good grasp of the overall principle, I think we still have lots to discover when it comes to the concrete practices that help us listen to the organization. I'm sure this is an area where we will see lots of experimentation in the years to come. Exciting times!

Practices are lifeless without the underlying worldview

In this book, I put the focus squarely on some of the concrete practices under the hood of Teal organizations. New practices are fundamental to reinventing organizations—you can't have self-management without a form of advice process; you can't have wholeness without safe space. Describing some of these concrete practices is the best way, I believe, to make this new organizational model tangible, to take the mystery out of what could otherwise look like a pipe dream or a utopia.

And yet, these practices only come to life if leaders espouse the worldview that underlies them. Many leaders looking at the world through more traditional, Orange lenses are frustrated by the so-called VUCA world (volatility, uncertainty, complexity, ambiguity). They look for fixes to make their organization more agile and their employees more motivated, and they could be tempted to adopt some of the practices in this book. I'm convinced this won't work. Every management practice comes with an underlying worldview (see page 35 for the example of compensation). A practice that isn't in tune with the leadership's worldview will quickly feel lifeless and might even make things worse, adding confusion and inviting cynicism.

Interestingly, none of the founders or CEOs of organizations I researched chose to adopt Teal principles because they were looking to become more innovative and more agile, or because they wanted to boost income and reduce costs. They acted out of some kind of inner imperative. Management as we know

it simply didn't feel right for them. Some suspected that the new ways of operating should be more powerful and effective, but that wasn't the starting point. They were simply looking for ways to run their organization that would be aligned with who they are, with how they want things to be. And in the process, they have helped a new, coherent organizational model emerge that is inspiring people all over the world to imagine a more powerful, soulful, and purposeful future.

OK, I implemented every practice you write about! How soon until the profits start to rise??

So ...
... how do
we get there?

PART 3

I hope the previous pages have given you a sense of what Teal organizations are like. Perhaps, you've even developed a sense of how you'd feel working in such a place. In this part of the book, we'll address questions such as:

- What does it take for an organization to be Teal?
- What is the role of leadership in such an organization?
- If you start a new organization, what might be some of the practices you would include from day one?
- And if you feel inspired to transform an existing, traditional organization, how might you go about it?

Necessary conditions

From the research, I've concluded that there are two—and only two—necessary conditions for organizations to make the leap to Teal structures and practices:

1 Top leadership: The founder or the top leader (let's call her the CEO for lack of a better term) must view the world through Teal lenses; she must have grown into that perspective, or Teal management practices won't make sense to her. Case examples show that it is helpful, but not necessary, to have several other senior leaders also operating in a Teal manner.

2 Ownership: Owners of the organization and their representatives must also understand and embrace a Teal worldview. Experience shows that board members who "don't get it" can temporarily give a Teal leader free rein when their methods deliver outstanding results. But when the organization hits a rough patch or faces a critical choice, owners will want to get things under control in the only way that makes sense to them—through top-down, hierarchical control mechanisms. This happened at two of the twelve organizations I researched.

Take the case of AES, an electric power company. Its first twenty years were spectacularly successful. In less than twenty years, it grew from zero to forty thousand employees operating power plants in more than thirty countries on five continents. In 2001, in the wake of the Enron collapse and the 9/11 attacks, its stock price plummeted, just like all other electricity producers. Board members became extremely nervous and insisted on reinstating control mechanisms and hierarchy at all levels. When Dennis Bakke, AES's founder, refused, they forced a Co-CEO onto him. After a few months, Bakke resigned in frustration. A similar story happened at BSO/Origin, a ten thousand-person IT consulting firm that originated in the Netherlands. It had had a very successful track record based on a large degree of self-management, but when it was acquired by Philips in 1994, the new owner quickly insisted on traditional management methods, and the company lost its mojo.

If I'm right that these two conditions are necessary for a real transformation to Teal, then I know that I'm dashing the hopes of people who work in organizations where these conditions are not in place. (Later in this chapter we will discuss what someone can nevertheless do—say, as a middle manager—in such a case.) But seen from another angle, this means that no other parameter is truly critical. Sometimes I get asked if some sectors might be off-limits for Teal—for instance, highly regulated sectors like banking. I don't believe that to be the case. AES has operated power plants based on the advice process, and the energy sector is one of the most highly regulated.

Geography and cultural backgrounds seem not to matter much either. It is true that the twelve companies I researched have their roots in the West (Europe and the United States), but several of them have plants and subsidiaries in Asia, Africa, or Latin America, and their practices seem to work there just as well. Certain cultures tend to be more deferent and hierarchical than others, but I believe that the longing for self-management or wholeness taps into deep, fundamental human yearnings. That seems to be confirmed by the many emails I have received from literally all corners of the world where people tell me how much they resonate with Teal oranizational practices.

Starting a Teal organization from scratch

As you read this book, you are perhaps about to start a new business, nonprofit, school, or hospital. And you wonder how to bake Teal yeast into the dough of the organization from the start. Rejoice! It's easier to start a Teal organization from scratch than to transform an existing organization already set in its ways. And, most likely, it will make your journey more powerful and joyful. But next to everything else going on, it's time to be extra mindful: by default, you are likely to simply reproduce today's management practices. You must now catch yourself in the act and consciously choose a new, less familiar, path.

One of the first questions I'd invite you to ponder is simply this: *what resonates most deeply with you of the things you've read so far about Teal organizations?* If you want to go a step further: *what is it in you, in your history, that vibrates, that excites you (as much as it scares you, perhaps) at the prospect of doing this?* I know that some people resonate strongly with self-management, for instance, because something deep inside them finds it painful that so many people don't get to express their talents in life. Others resonate with some aspects of wholeness, because they long for a place where they can drop the mask and connect with people at a deeper level. Others are so taken by their organization's purpose that they truly want to listen, to be of service. If you listen within, what moves you?

Another question: *if for a moment you try to take yourself (your wishes, your dreams) out of the equation and listen to the budding organization, what is the purpose that it wants to serve? What form and shape will best serve its purpose?* Let these questions drive what you want to do. I believe you are much more likely to reach your purpose powerfully and smoothly (well, somewhat more smoothly, let's be realistic!) if you let yourself be guided from within than if you pursue some mental construct of what a Teal organization should be like.

Creating a Teal organization is not a box-ticking exercise where you simply adopt a list of new practices. That said, there *are* some practices that are foundational. If you feel self-management is the way to go, then by any means, start with people having *multiple roles* instead of job titles. Use the *advice process* and determine a *conflict resolution mechanism*. These are probably the three most important ingredients to start with, and you'll define the next ones as you go.

If wholeness is important to you, some of the foundational practices might be for you and your team to explore which *ground rules* you want to

establish to create a safe space; to choose some soulful *meeting practices*; and to determine *recruitment* and *onboarding processes* that will help new colleagues join the groove. Perhaps you want to make sure you listen to the organization's evolutionary purpose from day one. Often we feel we need to have detailed business plans and budgets when we start a new venture. Ask yourselves: *what's the (minimal) amount of planning the project really needs? And what is simply guessing in the dark to have an illusion of control? Can I let go of it so I stay open to signals, to new opportunities?* Of course, many banks or venture capitalists still believe in predict-and-control more than sense-and-respond and often insist on detailed plans, and you might need to make some to give them a sense of comfort.

Transforming
an existing organization

The question I get asked most often these days is: "How can I transform my existing organization?" Jean-François Zobrist (the CEO who helped the brass foundry and automotive supplier FAVI adopt self-management) always replies to this question with the shortest of answers:

Démerdez-vous

I'm too polite to translate this literally, but it means something like, "You go figure it out!" What he wants to say, in his own provocative style, is: there is no recipe. If you are serious about this, you'll find a way. You are smart and resourceful enough to figure it out. You won't get everything right, but a way will open. I agree with him. There is no recipe. And I've come to believe that if the CEO really wants this (and if the board lets him— remember the second necessary condition), it will happen. We know it can be done. FAVI did it. AES acquired dozens of traditionally run power plants all over the world and managed, time and time again, to transform them. And since the book *Reinventing Organizations* came out, I have heard from many organizations that are making the leap to Teal. The simplest lesson I've learned from this is that every journey is truly unique. Which is, I guess, a fig leaf to say: these are early days. We don't

137

know much yet about how such journeys unfold, as most companies are still in the middle of it. We simply lack in-depth research about it. So I can't offer any definitive answers when people ask me, "How can I transform my existing organization?" But I can nevertheless offer some insights into what you might expect and highlight some common misconceptions about the journey.

We need to upgrade how we think about change

Before you start the journey, it might be worthwhile to examine how you think about change in organizations. Like many people, you might have a mental model that stems from an Orange, mechanistic worldview ... that could do with upgrading! Let me lay a bit of groundwork: there is a difference between a *complex* and a *complicated* system. At FAVI, they have a great metaphor to explain the difference.

An airplane like a Boeing or an Airbus is a COMPLICATED system. There might be tens of thousands of parts, but they all respond to a linear logic. Take out a part at random, and an engineer will be able to tell you exactly if and how the plane will be impaired.

A bowl of spaghetti, on the other hand, is a COMPLEX system. It has only a few dozen parts, but tug at one end of a strand of spaghetti that sticks out, and even the most powerful computer in the world will not be able to predict what will happen.

Our dominant mental model for change comes with the hidden assumption that organizations are *complicated* systems, like an airplane. According to this model, if we are smart in our analysis, we can plan a change effort for the next two or even five years. And once we have a smart plan, it simply takes disciplined execution. The reality is that organizations are almost always *complex* systems. That's why so many large change efforts fail.

So how can you help a *complex* system transform? Just think carefully about the first step you want to take, and perhaps the second that might follow. And then listen carefully, in the spirit of sense-and-respond. To stay with the metaphor: if we want to untangle the spaghetti bowl, we start by looking at it from all sides, and when we think we have found the most promising strand of spaghetti to pull on, we start to do so carefully. If it keeps coming, we keep pulling. If we seem to hit a knot, then it's time to pause, take a good look again, and start pulling somewhere else.

The truth is that our organizations are so complex that however smart we are, we can't predict what will happen when we introduce even big changes. New, unexpected opportunities might open up that we can seize. And certainly some parts of the system will scream because something is out of balance. So let's start with the one or two changes that make most sense for now, and then listen carefully for the next change the system is calling for.

This requires a new stance from leaders, a stance that shows confidence and a strong commitment to the journey, as well as a willingness to say openly that any pretense of a comprehensive, up-front plan would be comforting, but an illusion. And that change is never entirely painless; for a while, things will be out of balance and confusing.

Some people will likely be unhappy about this and criticize you. They want you to protect them from pain and refuse to listen when you say: this is beyond anyone's power. Careful, though! I've seen leaders who've taken this insight too far and responded to any and all criticism with, "Pain is part of the transformation." This is interesting terrain for leaders: stay open for valid input, while learning to set aside the misguided criticisms that are coming your way.

What's the current level of psychological ownership?

Every organization starting a transformation to Teal is likely to wonder: *how fast or slow should I go? How much risk can we take?* The answer, I've come to understand, hinges on one critical variable—the level of psychological ownership people feel for their organization. If, before the transformation, most colleagues feel strongly about their work and their organization, you can go fast and can take quite a risk. In the midst of the transformation, when there is some confusion or even a bit of chaos, colleagues will rally, will self-organize to put new structures in place and save the day. If, on the other hand, employees have little emotional investment in the organization and in its purpose, when work is a burden to be minimized ... then don't be surprised if, when they are given freedom, they take the freedom but not the responsibility. So one of the key questions I invite you to ponder is simply the following:

What's the level of psychological ownership in your organization?

The way FAVI, a traditional, hierarchical factory, adopted self-management illustrates this well. Shortly after Jean-François Zobrist was hired from the outside as the new CEO, he tried to engage the members of his executive team to hand power over to machine operators, but they resisted the idea again and again. Nine months into his role as CEO he decided to change tactics. It was the last working day of the year, just before the factory would close for the Christmas break. People were cleaning up the factory, the machines already quiet, when he gathered everyone for an improvised address. Standing on top of a few pallets, he shared that the way workers were controlled in the company felt disgraceful to him.

"I've been here with you nine months. Nine months that I've seen what you do, that I see people with courage, great professionals who love their work, but whom we prevent from doing good work. I know that people like you don't need carrots and sticks."

Zobrist went on to name a few things that would change. No time clocks anymore. No more salary deductions for coming in late. The stock room would no longer be locked. No more separate dining room for managers, and so forth.

Zobrist finished by adding: "How will we operate in the future? In all honesty, I don't know. I'm convinced that you deserve that we work together differently, but I don't have an alternative model. I suggest that, together, we learn by doing, with good intentions, common sense, and in good faith."[18]

The factory had a system that incentivized the workers for the number of pieces they machined per hour. That system would be scrapped too, and what people used to make in terms of bonus would simply be added to the base pay.

Managers were aghast and complained loudly to Zobrist after the holidays. This was a recipe for disaster! Productivity would collapse! Zobrist admits he checked the productivity numbers every day for a week, wondering what would happen. It turned out that productivity didn't decrease but increased! What was going on? When you operate a machine, the operators told Zobrist, there is an optimal rhythm that is physiologically the least tiring for the body. In the old system, with the hourly targets, they had always intentionally slowed down. They gave themselves some slack in case management increased their targets. For years, operators had effectively worked at a rhythm that was more tiring for them and less profitable for the company!

The route that Zobrist chose to transform the factory isn't for the fainthearted. I'm not necessarily advising shock therapy as the only or best method of transformation. But FAVI's story illustrates the point about psychological ownership. From the moment he was appointed CEO, Zobrist walked the shop floor and spoke with the operators every day. Nine months later, he knew that they felt strongly about their factory, and he sensed that they trusted and respected him. After the Christmas bombshell, operators wanted to prove that he was right to trust them: they would rise to the occasion.

AES, which took over dozens of traditionally run power plants around the world, also understood the importance of trust before making big changes. Most often, the workforce they inherited was demotivated and distrustful of people at the top. After every acquisition, three or four leaders from AES took over key positions in the plant, including plant director, but they refrained from introducing AES's practices right away. They first sought to create real trust with people in the organization. It would often take a year, sometimes two, for frontline workers to sense that something was different about their new leadership and become invested in where the plant was going. Only then would bigger changes like the advice process be introduced.

Many ways to start

Here is another question that always comes up: where do we start? With the whole organization right away, or perhaps just in one part of it first? I've heard from organizations that have tried a variety of approaches, in ways that look equally promising. This might give you some food for thought for your own journey.

Many organizations chose to experiment and test new methods within one unit to learn and build excitement. The next question then becomes: which unit? Many criteria can be relevant to choosing a good candidate. I believe the most important one might simply be: which one has the most energy? Which unit has a leader who is raring to get started?

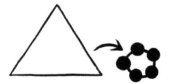

Jos de Blok is advising two direct competitors of Buurtzorg, and they've settled on a clever approach. Instead of transforming the existing organizations, they have built a separate, small Buurtzorg-inspired unit next to it. Nurses are allowed to jump ship, and the idea is for the new unit to grow, while the old one dies out.

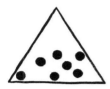

Some organizations choose to encourage experiments throughout the organization. This is the approach chosen, for instance, by the CEO of a sixty thousand-person global retailer. He sent out an open invitation to everyone in the organization to attend an event that marked the launch of the transformation. In no time, enthusiasts from all over the world registered. At the event, the CEO shared his vision and then encouraged everyone to experiment, to do a bit of mischief, to question how things are done, and to push the boundaries. The hope is to kick-start the transformation with lots of parallel experimentation and to generalize the best solutions that bubble up.

Another approach is to introduce/upgrade a certain practice for the entire organization at once. For instance, to adopt a new meeting practice to invite wholeness. Or to implement the advice process throughout the organization. Or to change the budgeting process. The best way to create momentum and buy in, it seems, is to have these new processes designed by a voluntary task force. Or even better, by a large group of colleagues using a process of collective intelligence such as Open Space or Appreciative Inquiry. The more people are involved in the design, the more easily everyone will adopt the new practices.

The four approaches outlined above can be mixed, of course. Remember the bowl of spaghetti: the best we can do is to look carefully at the organization and try to sense what would work best. But let's not overestimate our powers; we won't come up with a perfect plan. There might be some wisdom in testing a number of different approaches and seeing what unfolds. In some places, we'll witness unexpected bursts of energy, breaking up the old system much faster and more joyfully than we thought possible. And other experiments will run into the sand. While this is hard to predict, we can listen and react quickly, building on the successes and learning from the disappointments.

Following the energy

So where then exactly do you start? There are so many possible places to begin that I've seen some organizations almost paralyzed by the question. We are so used to thinking that we need to analyze everything in depth before taking action that making the first step can be difficult. Here are two thoughts that you might find helpful. Both have to do with listening, in the spirit of sense-and-respond.

The first is for the CEO to listen to her or his personal aspiration. *Deep inside, what are you yearning for? What change would be profoundly meaningful to you? Is it more in the field of self-management, of wholeness, of evolutionary purpose?* When you clarify this, some of the first steps might become obvious. Some of you might wonder about this emphasis on the CEO, when Teal is about distributing authority. There is indeed a profound paradox in the transformation process that we encounter again and again—to move away from existing practices in a pyramid, a committed and powerful CEO is needed. Therefore, rather than fighting the CEO's power, I believe we should welcome it for the benefit of the transformation.

And second, in parallel, let's listen to the organization. The key question here is: *for which change is there most energy? Where is energy currently blocked or waiting to be set free?* In some organizations, it might be a budget process that nobody believes in and that drains huge amounts of energy. Or it might be cumbersome approval mechanisms that slow everything down. Or a lack of meaning, of purpose. Or a transactional culture, where subtle fears keep everyone interacting from behind a mask. Whatever it is, this place might be the natural starting point. Simply follow the energy, and the change process might snowball, fueled by the vitality that is unleashed.

The importance of self-correction

In their transformation journey, many organizations itch to get rid of all the mechanisms of control that have been stifling and frustrating people: the thick book of rules and procedures, the approvals needed from higher ups, and so forth. But then what? Some people are comfortable betting everything on trust. Others feel nervous about the risks of just letting go. We need to understand, I believe, that in Teal, control is exerted in a whole new way. Let's first get a misunderstanding out of the way. Control is useful and necessary. Natural systems want control; our bodies, for instance, need the temperature to be within certain bounds, or we die! But nature doesn't implement control with rule books, hoping to stop any problem from happening. Control is embedded in the organization's capacity to self-correct. This is a notion we are hardly familiar with, but should be, because it is extraordinarily powerful.

Trying to insulate ourselves from risks up front is almost impossible. We can keep adding rules and approval mechanisms, but we'll never be fully safe. How could we ever foresee everything that could go wrong? What we know for sure will happen is that we'll asphyxiate creativity and initiative-taking. Therefore, for all but the most intolerable risks, let's not try and prevent things going wrong up front, but wonder instead: how quickly will a problem be detected, and will someone step up to correct it?[19]

Let's take a practical example: the policy for travel expenses. In many large organizations, there is a whole set of rules and approvals that stipulates who is allowed to travel, what kind of airline ticket you can buy, and what hotel you can stay in. Perhaps you yearn to get rid of it all. But if there is no more control whatsoever, will costs not spiral, well, out of control?

A common mistake is to get rid of existing control mechanisms without putting in place what's needed for systems to self-correct.

A global retail chain decided that employees would be trusted to book their travels without their managers having to approve, or even be informed, as a powerful symbol that times have changed. Within a few months, they realized that travel expenses had increased substantially. After some analysis, they realized that the increase was positive: it wasn't that everyone suddenly flew first class; people were taking more initiatives, which resulted in more travel. But among all the travel, there were a few situations that looked like possible abuses. Trust will always be abused at some point; that's part of life. The question is not should we keep trusting or stop trusting? Rather, it is: does our system have the ability to self-correct quickly or not? For a system to self-correct, three things are needed:

1 *A shared understanding of what's healthy.* A group of volunteers could determine some guidelines to help everyone in making their choices.

2 *Information,* i.e., the minimum data that is needed for problems to become quickly apparent, to be shared transparently throughout the organization.

3 And *a forum for conversation* to trigger self-corrective action. When there is data but no one talks about it, nothing will happen. To go back to our example: it takes courage for someone to step up to a colleague that travels first class when everyone else flies economy. That becomes much easier if there is a forum—say a quarterly meeting where team members review information on travel expenses and address any issues.

Whenever you get rid of an important mechanism of control, be mindful about these three conditions so that the organization can self-correct. And if you forget, well, you can trust that at some point the system will self-correct ... even its own lack of self-correction! This is what happened in the case of the global retail chain: it now has put in place transparency around travel expenses and forums to discuss the data.

How will colleagues react and adapt? Some things you can expect ...

There is an interesting finding I've heard very consistently from organizations that embark on a journey to Teal: their predictions of who would champion the transformation, and who would likely resist it, are often far off the mark. Some people who were passive and even cynical suddenly blossom and surprise everyone with all sorts of initiatives. And others, who were seen as natural champions, struggle unexpectedly. The consequence is that it's best to kick-start the journey with open invitations and see who bites, even when your instinct tells you to launch the initiative with a few people you trust will be champions.

Another theme that comes back consistently from companies embracing self-management is that people at the bottom of the pyramid will embrace the changes quite quickly if they trust you and if there is enough psychological ownership. On the other hand, most senior and middle managers, as well as people in staff functions, will view the transition to self-management as a threat (at least at first). Don't expect them to embrace self-management with hoorays. In the best of cases, they will lose the only way they could wield their hierarchical power. More likely, their function

will disappear altogether and they may have to find themselves a new job—within the organization or outside it. At FAVI, Zobrist dealt with it gracefully: he made it clear that teams would self-manage and that there would be no more need for supervisors, managers, and many of the staff functions. No one would be fired, but it wasn't his role to find people new jobs. He suggested that they take their time, look around, talk with colleagues, and find or create themselves a role in which they could add value. Think about it: most companies have many more ideas and projects than they have resources. Suddenly some of the smartest people are freed and can pursue these ideas. Some people might prefer to take a management position in another company, and they can be supported financially in that transition.

Managers who stay often experience phantom pain at first. The old way to exert power is no longer there; they must learn new ways to make things happen. But quite consistently, those who stay report after some time how liberating it is to no longer have the pressure of bosses to please and subordinates to motivate and keep in line. They can finally go back to doing creative work.

The role of the "CEO"

There is often some confusion, I've noticed, about the role of the "CEO" in Teal organizations. Is there even such a thing? CEOs who make the leap often wonder what their role should be in the transformation and beyond. You might have noticed that the organizations I discuss all have pretty formidable founders or leaders—Jos de Blok at Buurtzorg, Jean-François Zobrist at FAVI, Chris Rufer at Morning Star, and so forth. How is that compatible with self-management? How can there still be a CEO when there is no pyramid? Let's look at this carefully: this is one more area where we need to reprogram ourselves, to grow into a new perspective.

Remember, the goal is not to make everyone equal (see page 78), but to make everyone fully powerful. Jos de Blok and Chris Rufer have to play by the same rules as everyone else. For instance, unlike a traditional CEO, they can't impose anything; they must use the advice process. But the goal is not to cut them down to size—how would that serve the organization?—but to use their talents, skills, and energy as well as possible, just like everyone else's.

Almost all of the organizations I researched stopped using job titles. Instead, everyone holds a number of granular roles. In a team of nurses at Buurtzorg, you might recall, there is no team leader. The various roles such as "leader" have been distributed among team members. One team member might do holiday planning and recruiting, while another looks at the financials and a third one manages the relationship with the local hospital. In the same way, we must stop thinking about the CEO as one job, but look more granularly at the underlying roles.

Not one but many roles ...

Many of the traditional roles of the CEO fall away—there are, for example, no targets to set, no budgets to approve, no executive team to chair, no promotions to decide on. There are two traditional roles that "CEOs" (for lack of a better word) often retain (but these roles could just as well be distributed to other colleagues):

- One is to be the *public face* of the organization to the outside world, because clients, vendors, and regulators often expect to be able to talk with the big boss. The "CEO" can play this role inside too, for instance, participating in the onboarding process with all new joiners to share with them some of the organization's history, values, and purpose.
- Another is to be a *sensor* of where the organization wants to go. Of course, everyone in the organization is invited to be a sensor! But in many cases, people in the organization recognize the founder's or "CEO's" ability to sense and articulate where the journey is going with particular clarity and are happy for the "CEO" to play that role.[20]

A new role: holding the space

Here is a new role that comes into play. Teal operating principles run deeply against the grain of accepted management thinking. A critical role of the founder/"CEO" is therefore to "hold the space" for Teal structures and practices. Whenever a problem comes up, someone, somewhere, will call for tried-and-proven solutions: *let's add a rule, a control system; let's put the issue under some centralized function; let's make processes more prescriptive; let's make such decisions at a higher level in the future.* The calls can come from different corners—one time it's a board member who will call for more control, another time a colleague or a client. Over and over again, the CEO must ensure that the new practices are reaffirmed and that traditional management methods don't creep in through the back door. Two small examples from FAVI illustrate this well.

Unlocking the storeroom was a symbolic step early in the transformation of the factory. Machine operators no longer needed to get their supervisors to sign off for a new pair of safety gloves. Then one day, a drill was stolen, and predictably, some people felt the right response was to tighten control.

Zobrist did none of that. Instead, he simply sent a message to everyone.

That's all it took to solve the problem. The stolen drill remained an isolated incident, and the storeroom stayed unlocked.

Zobrist reacted in a similar fashion on the day a female colleague reported the drawing of a penis on a wall in the women's bathroom. Some people were offended and called for an investigation. In his customary cheeky style, Zobrist put up a flipchart in front of the women's bathroom and wrote on it:

There is among us a slightly deranged person who feels the need to make sexual drawings for his or her sanity. Please make your drawings on this paper in the future and not on the bathroom walls.

Just like with the drill, the issue didn't reappear. These are small incidents, but we need to be careful nevertheless: the temptation is big to seek safety from harm through good old methods of control. There are, of course, more complicated issues—for instance when a regulator insists on certain control mechanisms, or when certain software packages are designed for a hierarchical work flow and authorizations. *Holding the space* in these cases often calls for unusual solutions. AES was publicly listed on Wall Street, a status that comes with the imposition that only colleagues identified as "insiders" get to see internal information that could influence the stock price. But AES's form of self-management relied on information being shared widely. Therefore, instead of a mere handful of "insiders" as at a typical listed company, AES had ... thousands and thousands! All were subject to "blackout periods," which normally only apply to senior executives, during which they could not trade the company securities.

Role modeling self-management, wholeness, and evolutionary purpose

Another specific role that founders and "CEOs" of Teal organizations must take on is to role model, to the best of their ability, the behaviors needed for self-management, wholeness, and evolutionary purpose to flourish. Take wholeness: there is little chance that people will take the risk of showing up in the fullness of who they are if the founder or "CEO" is hiding behind a professional mask. Tami Simon, the founder and leader of Sounds True, gives the example of bringing depth to check-ins at the beginning of meetings:

"Check-ins can have different levels of depth to them. People can check in and say, 'Yeah, I'm doing great, everything is fine.' I find you need someone in the room who will go to a deeper level inside themself. … It doesn't take very many people; it can take just one or two. I'm always willing to be that person."[1]

For the rest, a colleague like any other

Once organizations embrace self-management, the former "CEOs" suddenly find themselves with lots of time on their hands! They were previously tied to back-to-back meetings, often booked weeks in advance to approve decisions. Now decision-making is distributed throughout the company. This was brought home to me powerfully when I visited Sun Hydraulics, a Florida-based company that designs and manufactures hydraulic valves and manifolds. When I met Allen Carlson, the company's CEO, I asked him if he would show me his agenda for the week. Now, mind you, Sun Hydraulics is a NASDAQ-listed company, with subsidiaries in Germany, the UK, and Korea. And yet, he had only four meetings planned the entire week ... two of which were with me! The same phenomenon plays out with many organizations that are currently making the leap. Several "CEOs" have told me almost exactly the same story: I took three weeks of holiday, and I didn't receive a single call from the office!

So what do founders and "CEOs" do then? Part of their time will go into the four roles

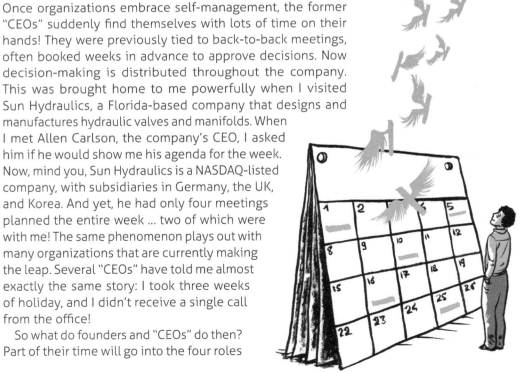

we discussed (being the public face, sensing, holding the space, role modeling). This often leaves them with much time on their hands, which they use in creative work. Like any other colleague, they can take on an initiative or join someone else's. They can fill an operational role that fits their talents and interests. I hear from CEOs who tell me that this has been deeply satisfying at a personal level. Just as much as everyone else, they are often very creative people, but they didn't have space to express their creativity in all the years they were traditional CEOs.

If you are not the CEO, what can you do?

I've had quite a few conversations with people who want to adopt Teal practices in their work, but their CEO isn't really into these ideas. For that reason, a wholesale transformation of the organization is not on the table. The CEO won't embrace practices that make no sense from his or her perspective. If, nevertheless, you want to somehow help the whole organization become a better place, instead of aiming "vertically" for Teal, your energy is better spent, I would suggest, going for "horizontal" changes: moving, for instance, from an unhealthy version of Orange to a healthier one. Orange organizations can be vibrant and innovative places where management by objectives gives people room to maneuver and to express themselves; or they can be stressful, disheartening places constrained by a thicket of rules, procedures, budgets, and arbitrary targets. As a middle or senior manager, you can champion changes that make sense from an Orange perspective and that your top management can embrace (say, more agile, client-facing units).

At a local level, there is more you can do than you might suspect

Within your area, for the people working "below" you, many more possibilities open up. For instance, take all the practices related to wholeness. If you bring them in wisely (and by invitation of course; no one can be forced into wholeness) they will probably fly below the radar screen of leaders at the very top. Executives there might hear about it and find it a bit strange, but if it makes people happy and keeps them motivated, what is there to say?

When it comes to self-management and evolutionary purpose, you'll more quickly bump into the rest of the organization. Taking away the hierarchical structure altogether, for instance, would set off alarm bells around the company, but there are things you can do nevertheless. You can introduce the advice process in your teams. Or you can change the appointment process. Take the case where one of your direct reports has changed jobs and must be replaced.

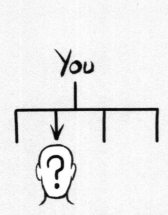

Instead of you interviewing candidates and naming a successor ...

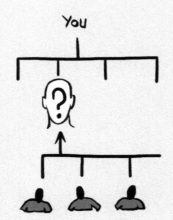

... why don't you let people one level below write the profile of their future boss, do the interviews, and select the person?

Experience shows that people put the bar very high and do a great job when it comes to picking their boss. And the new boss starts walking on water: all her subordinates want her to succeed to prove they made the right choice.

This new practice is more than symbolic; it changes the power hierarchy between a manager and the direct reports in profound ways. You can add more to the mix (unless HR policies really tie your hands behind your back): for the yearly appraisal discussions, you can do it in a peer-based fashion (see page 107) rather than the traditional boss–subordinate one-on-one. Perhaps you can even introduce peer-based practices for people working "below" you to decide on salary increases and bonuses. All of these changes—how decisions are made, how people are appointed, evaluated, and compensated—can release lots of energy. Managers can no longer control people by fear and must engage in more meaningful ways of collaborating. And yet, to the outside world, the pyramid looks reassuringly intact.

A middle manager I once met called it "opening the shit umbrella": you participate in the practices that come from higher up the hierarchy, but you don't cascade them down. You might even be able to do this for something like budgets and targets. Say the budget process in your company has become largely meaningless. While you'll have to play the game with your superiors, you can perhaps stop it at your level and ask the people who work for you to engage in a more productive, life-giving way of visualizing the future.

How long will you stay?
And what risks are you willing to take?

There are two questions I'd invite you to ask yourself before introducing such changes. A first question is: *how long will you realistically stay in your current position?* If you believe that in a year or two you might move elsewhere, it's probably not wise to go too radical. Unless your successor happens to be a pioneer like you, he's likely to return to business as usual, and people on your teams might feel cheated. Are you willing to stay for, say, five years in that position? Would you be willing to forgo a promotion that might come your way?

The second question has to do with the risks you are willing to take. Listen inside and ask yourself: *are you willing, if it comes to it, to be branded as someone who colors very much outside the lines? Are you willing, possibly, to lose your job over this?* I'm not suggesting you should, but it's helpful to know how risk averse you are, to help you decide how bold you can be.

I regularly have conversations with people who tell me they've had it, they want to resign from their job as middle or senior managers. I like to inquire in return: "If you want to leave anyway because the current management paradigm isn't working for you, why don't you, in your sphere of influence, make all the changes you want to do? I mean, what's the worst thing that could happen—that you lose your job? That's what you just told me you were going for." Of course, everyone's story is unique, and I can't possibly know what the person in front of me is called to do. But I think it's worthwhile exploring that possibility. This journey might prove to be one of much learning, and who knows? Your identity, how people view you, might change in the process, and you might meet many interesting people. Perhaps this might be the best way to launch you on the next step in your life's journey.

There is a simpler way[22]

At some point, after the book *Reinventing Organizations* came out, I realized that there are two very different ways to talk about all this. One story is that Teal is cutting-edge stuff, that few people really understand it, that transforming the organization will be risky and require lots of time and energy. This is the story that most of us intuitively go for.

And then there is a whole other way to look at it: that Teal practices are the simpler, more intuitive, more natural, way to do things. That most of us long to work in natural hierarchies, long for communities where we can bring in our whole selves, long for a purpose that gives guidance and meaning. That really, we'll end up, after going through an (un)learning curve, with a simpler way to go about work.

Let's illustrate these two stories with the example of organizational structures. We can look at self-management and say: *wow, how will we ever operate without the pyramid? That must be so complicated!* And then there is another way to think about it. Let me try to express this in a visual way. At Morning Star, once a year, every employee formalizes agreements with the people they work most closely with. (In essence: This is what I commit to and that you can expect of me. Do you agree with this?) This graph depicts these agreements at Morning Star.

Every dot is a person, and every line a formalized agreement that two colleagues have with each other. This, you could say, is Morning Star's organization chart. Actually, this is what every organization's *real* org chart looks like. This is how work gets done.

But then, we force an alien structure onto the natural way to get things done, which distorts and complicates everything. So really, which structure is simpler: the pyramid, or a self-managing structure? The answer, I believe, is that the pyramid is easier to comprehend, because we are so used to it. But an organic structure is much simpler, much more natural and intuitive. It's there anyway, always fluid and evolving, so let's recognize it and work with it. And not try to add a second one on top of it.

The same holds true for any of the practices in Teal. None of them is complicated; no rocket science is involved. Take the advice process: isn't it obvious, in some way, that you should ask advice from people who know something about the subject, and from those who will have to live with your decision? Isn't that what you would do naturally, if you tried to come up with the best decision? Remember the story of Jos de Blok and the twenty-four-hour decision cycle (page 70): how much simpler is this than the cumbersome way we often practice hierarchical decision-making? Or remember Morning Star's self-set salary increases (page 75): it's wonderfully simple, and it cuts through all the haggling and complaining about compensation.

The same is true for wholeness: we can tell stories about how it's hard to get colleagues to show up whole in the work place. And yet, as soon as you create a truly safe space, time and time again people start showing up in more profound, more authentic ways, as if they had been waiting for this for a long time. None of the wholeness practices requires a master's degree. Learning to use tingsha bells in meetings (page 104) doesn't take more than five minutes to explain.

So which story to believe? I think there is truth in both. Teal practices are surprisingly simple, much simpler than the management methods we are used to. But there is real unlearning involved in order to reach simplicity. You could say that for our generation, the journey to Teal organizations is mostly one of unlearning complicated ways for doing what can be much simpler.

This is just the beginning

Many of us feel that today's management is broken. Thanks to extraordinary pioneers—the founders of Buurtzorg, RHD, Morning Star, Heiligenfeld, AES, FAVI, and others—we have a sense of the possibilities that could open up when we build organizations not as machines, but as living systems, seeking inspiration from nature and evolution. More that just a sense, we have a grasp of the structures, practices, and cultures that can help us bring to life powerful, soulful, and purposeful businesses, nonprofits, schools, and hospitals.

All of this is still very much emerging, of course; by no means do I believe we have seen everything there is to come. As more people and more organizations follow in the pioneers' footsteps, they will enrich and refine our understanding of this emerging model by pushing the boundaries and inventing new practices.

I'm only half-comfortable using the term "organizational model" because it could be read in a prescriptive, monolithic way, as a list of structures and practices that must be rigidly implemented. I no longer believe that we need to design and shape organizations in the way we design machines and buildings—objectively, from the outside. What we can do is seek inspiration from these pioneers to evoke new ways of being, new ways of operating, from within an organization. Ultimately, it comes down to the living system of *your* organization, and of you within it. What does the living system—what do *you*—feel called to do, to become?

These are extraordinary times to be alive. Often confusing, but full of possibilities. It is up to us to invent a new path. There is an old saying, sometimes attributed to Native American tribes, that seems particularly relevant to me as we embark on this shift to more life-giving organizations:

"We are the people we have been waiting for."

Here are some resources if you want to go deeper

The book *Reinventing Organizations* is starting to turn into a movement, with people in organizations of all stripes deciding to make the leap to Teal. Exciting times! A series of projects has grown out of this movement, and more are in the making. In some ways, a whole little ecosystem is arising from the book, providing practical support to people in organizations making the leap. Here are some of them. For a longer list that's up to date, check **reinventingorganizations.com/resources**.

Reinventing Organizations

Of course, the book *Reinventing Organizations* goes into both more breadth and more depth than this illustrated version does. It has a list of suggested readings at the end if you want to explore some more.

Wiki

More than one hundred readers came together to create a knowledge wiki. Each of the Teal practices has its own article that sometimes goes into much more depth than the book ever could. Say you want to create an advice-based compensation system—you'll find in the wiki quite detailed discussions on the topic and practical examples. The goal of the wiki is always to stay up-to-date with the latest thinking, outgrowing the book over time.
reinventingorganizationswiki.com

News hub

Two readers, who were quickly joined by more, created *Enlivening Edge*, a newsletter and website that aims to share and reference the news in the space of organizations going "Teal." It's a great resource to stay current and be encouraged with what's unfolding.
enliveningedge.org

Conversation platform

A number of leaders making the journey to transform their organizations wanted to connect with like-minded peers. We set up an online conversation platform, where they discuss with and learn from one another.
discourse.reinventingorganizations.com

Meetups

In an increasing number of cities, people organize meetups or communities of practice to share and get inspiration and support from one another. Search online to find a group, or simply start one of your own.

Find your tribe

There are many more resources than the ones related to *Reinventing Organizations* that I just highlighted. We are currently witnessing a real outburst of activity in this field. Sometimes, an idea is ripe, a thought is ready to be thought. Perhaps you know the story of calculus being discovered in the seventeenth century not just by one person, but by at least two. Leibnitz and Newton both discovered calculus at the same time, while others like Fermat were onto it too. It's extraordinary, come to think of it: for 100,000 years of human history, no one had bothered with calculus. But suddenly something was in the air, and it resulted in a leap for science.

This is what's happening today with management and organizations. The founders of many of the organizations I researched tuned into something that is in the air, and so are thousands more right now. *Reinventing Organizations* is but one expression, one way to look at what's unfolding. There are many more people and budding movements tapping into the same field.

For instance, *Agile* and *Scrum* are two related movements that are fundamentally transforming the world of IT by bringing self-management and a form of sense-and-respond to programming projects. *Holacracy* is an elaborate, packaged "operating system" for self-management. It comes with a steep learning curve and a language that can be off-putting at first, but many organizations who stick with the system swear by it. *Sociocracy* is an earlier system for self-management that inspired Holacracy and that has its own following. There are academics who have created communities around related ideas—Otto Scharmer with *Theory U* and *U.Lab*, Robert Kegan with *Deliberately Developmental Organizations,* and Gary Hamel with the *MIX*, to name just a few.

These are just some of the bigger movements, but it seems like no week passes by without someone coining a framework to give words to what's unfolding, without a conference that explores new ways to be at work, without an organization that steps forward sharing how it has reinvented itself, without a new book on the topic. Exciting times. Something is in the air. In the midst of this all, I encourage you to find your own sources of inspiration, your own tribe.

Notes

1

A great number of researchers from many different fields have studied human evolution. Abraham Maslow famously looked at how human needs evolve along the human journey, from basic physiological needs to self-actualization. Others looked at development through the lenses of worldviews (Gebser, for instance), cognitive capacities (Piaget), values (Graves), moral development (Kohlberg, Gilligan), self-identity (Loevinger), spirituality (Fowler), leadership (Cook-Greuter, Kegan, Torbert), and so on.

In their exploration, they found consistently that humanity evolves in stages. We are not like trees that grow continuously. We evolve by sudden transformations, like a caterpillar that becomes a butterfly, or a tadpole a frog. Our knowledge about the stages of human development is now very robust. Two thinkers in particular—Ken Wilber and Jenny Wade—have done remarkable work comparing and contrasting all the major stage models and have discovered strong convergence. Every model might look at one side of the mountain (one looks at needs, another at cognition, for instance), but it's the same mountain. They may give different names to the stages or sometimes subdivide or regroup them differently. But the underlying phenomenon is the same, just like Fahrenheit and Celsius recognize—with different labels—that there is a point at which water freezes and another where it boils. This developmental view has been backed up by solid evidence from large pools of data; academics like Jane Loevinger, Susanne Cook-Greuter, Bill Torbert, and Robert Kegan have tested this stage theory with thousands and thousands of people in several cultures and in organizational and corporate settings, among others.

The way I portray the stages borrows from many researchers, and primarily from Wade's and Wilber's meta-analyses. It touches briefly upon different facets of every stage—the worldview, the needs, the cognitive development, the moral development. I refer to every stage, and to the corresponding organizational model, with both a name and a color. Naming the stages is always a struggle; a single adjective will never be able to capture all of the complex reality of a stage of human consciousness. I've chosen adjectives that I feel are the most evocative for each stage, in some cases borrowing a label from an existing stage theory, in other cases choosing a label of my own making. Integral Theory often refers to stages not with a name but with a color. Certain people find this color-coding to be highly memorable, and for that reason I'll often refer to a stage throughout this book with the corresponding color (which should not obscure the fact—let's add this to avoid any misunderstanding—that the way I describe the stages of consciousness stems from a personal synthesis of the work of different scholars, which while generally compatible might not always square entirely with the way Integral Theory describes the same stages, nor with the work of Clare Graves, that Spiral Dynamics has made popular using a similar color scheme).

2

This stage corresponds to Loevinger's and Cook-Greuter's "Self-protective," Kegan's "Imperial," Torbert's "Opportunistic," Graves' "CP," Spiral Dynamics' "Red," Piaget's "Pre-operational (Conceptual)," Wade's "Egocentric," and others.

3

According to Wikipedia, the idea of an aggressively dominant "alpha wolf" in gray wolf packs has been discredited by wolf biologists and researchers, and so-called "alphas" in packs are merely the breeding animals. This news makes for an interesting discussion. If in the past, we have projected a story of dominance onto the role of the alpha male in wolf packs, it is probably because we as human beings have long functioned this way. That researchers fairly recently began to see more subtle relationships in wolf packs might reveal that we ourselves are coming to operate from more complex worldviews. (Another intriguing possibility is that it would be the other way around: that researchers seeing the world today through Green lenses don't want to see alpha behavior and project their pluralistic stance onto the wolves. The trouble is: we really see the world not as it is, but as we are.)

4

The term "Conformist" is used by Loevinger, Cook-Greuter, and Wade, among others. This stage corresponds to Gebser's "Mythical," Loevinger's and Cook-Greuter's "Conformist," Graves' "DQ," Spiral Dynamics' "Blue," Kegan's "Interpersonal," Torbert's "Diplomat" and "Expert," Piaget's "Concrete Operational," and others.

5

The term "Achievement" is borrowed from Wade. This stage corresponds to Gebser's "Mental," Loevinger's and Cook-Greuter's "Self-Aware" and "Conscientious," Kegan's "Institutional," Torbert's "Achiever," Piaget's "Formal Operational," Graves' "ER," Spiral Dynamics' "Orange," and others; it is often simply referred to as modernity.

6

This stage corresponds to Loevinger's and Cook-Greuter's "Individualistic," Torbert's "Individualist," Wade's "Affiliative," Graves' "FS," Spiral Dynamics' "Green," and others; it is often simply referred to as postmodernity.

7

The first major study dates from 1992, when Harvard Business School professors John Kotter and James Heskett investigated this link in their book *Corporate Culture and Performance*. They established that companies with strong business cultures and empowered managers/employees outperformed other companies on revenue growth (by a factor of four), stock price increase (by a factor of eight), and increase in net income (by a factor of more than seven hundred) during the eleven years considered in the research. The book *Conscious Capitalism*, written by Raj Sisodia and John Mackey, has a whole chapter with references of similar studies to which interested readers can refer.

Any research trying to make such general claims as the superior outcome of one organizational model over another is bound to hit methodological limitations: the risk of selection bias is real (how do you "objectively" select which company is, say, "Green" or culture driven?); it's almost impossible to filter out the many factors other than the management model that determine an organization's success (the quality of the strategy, of the business model, of the assets, of the people, the patents, and so forth; not to mention sheer good luck); and on a principled level, one could question shareholder return or growth as the primary metric to gauge success, as most studies do. Perhaps direct experience ultimately matters more than academic claims. Anyone who spends time in organizations such as Southwest Airlines will return convinced that empowered workers in values-driven companies will on average outperform their peers in more traditional settings.

8

This stage corresponds to Gebser's "Integral," Loevinger's "Integrated," Cook-Greuter's "Construct-Aware," Kegan's "Interindividual," Torbert's "Strategist" and "Alchemist," Graves' "AN," Spiral Dynamics' "Yellow," Maslow's "Self-actualization," Wade's "Authentic," and others; it is often referred to as integral.

9

Ernst & Young, *Maatschappelijke Business Case (mBC) Buurtzorg Nederland, versie 1.1* (Netherlands: 2009).

10

According to Wikipedia, flocking is a collective animal behavior exhibited by many living beings such as birds, fish, bacteria, and insects. It is considered an emergent behavior arising from simple rules that are followed by individuals and does not involve any central coordination. Flocking behavior was first simulated on a computer in 1987 by Craig Reynolds. Basic models of flocking behavior are controlled by three simple rules:
1 Separation - avoid crowding neighbors (short-range repulsion)
2 Alignment - steer towards average heading of neighbors
3 Cohesion - steer towards average position of neighbors (long-range attraction)
With these three simple rules, flock moves are simulated in an extremely realistic way.

11

Dennis Bakke, who has long championed the advice process, wrote two books I recommend for anyone wanting to understand the transformative power of this decision-making method. *Joy at Work* traces the story of AES, a highly successful energy firm operating with the "advice process" in the 1980s and 1990s with forty thousand people in more than thirty countries. *The Decision Maker* is a business fable, a story of a fictional company's transformation when it embraces the advice process.

12

Daniel Pink's *Drive* provides a good overview of research on the matter.

13

Productivity at Buurtzorg is defined as the ratio of hours billed to the social security system over working hours. A ratio of 60 percent is deemed healthy for Buurtzorg. So if nurses in a team bill on average twenty-four hours of a forty-hour week (the rest is training, team meetings, commute, and so forth), Buurtzorg is in a healthy financial situation.

14

A similar effect is at play in schools where babies are brought into the classroom. Mary Gordon, a Canadian educator, pioneered a program where mothers (or fathers) and their babies come to spend time with a class of children at regular times. The results have been so spectacular that the program has by now been brought to thousands of classrooms in Canada, the United States, England, New Zealand, and elsewhere. David Bornstein wrote in *The New York Times*:

> *"Tough kids smile, disruptive kids focus, shy kids open up. The baby seems to act like a heart-softening magnet. ... 'Empathy can't be taught, but it can be caught,' Gordon often says—and not just by children. 'Programmatically my biggest surprise was that not only did empathy increase in children, but it increased in their teachers,' she added. 'And that, to me, was glorious, because teachers hold such sway over children.' Scientific studies with randomized control trials have shown extraordinary reductions in 'proactive aggression'—the deliberate and cold-blooded aggression of bullies who prey on vulnerable kids—as well as 'relational aggression'— things like gossiping, excluding others, and backstabbing."* (David Bornstein, "Fighting Bullying with Babies," Opinionator, *The New York Times*, November 8, 2010.)

15

The number of participants is also limited by the size of the largest meeting room in Bad Kissingen. Employees in Waldmünchen, two hundred miles away, are meeting at the same time, and the two assemblies form a single meeting thanks to oversized videoconference displays on both ends.

16

So much so that the company is about to shift to a biweekly rhythm—there simply aren't that many hot topics popping up anymore.

17

An organization that is cash strapped might also do a budget, to make sure its expenses and investments don't put it at risk. It's the same principle: let's make a budget if it provides real guidance for important decisions, but not to try to predict and control. Buurtzorg offers an interesting illustration of this. Teams at Buurtzorg don't do any significant purchasing or investments, so they don't bother with financial budgets at all. At the aggregate level, though, Buurtzorg makes a simple projection of its expected cash flow to get a sense of how many new teams it can allow to start up. New teams can take up to a year to break even, and given Buurtzorg's very rapid growth, it wants to make sure it doesn't go bust if too many new teams get started at the same time. The budget is exceedingly simple and fits on a single sheet of paper.

18

Zobrist, Jean-François. *La belle histoire de FAVI: L'entreprise qui croit que l'Homme est bon. Tome 1, Nos Belles Histoires.* (Paris: Humanisme et Organisations, 2008), p. 38.

19

Let's stay with the analogy of body temperature to bring this to life. Our body is able to adapt to a great range of outside temperatures and to the fact that we might do intense physical activity sometimes and be absolutely still at others. How does the body maintain its temperature, instead of overheating? The hypothalamus in the brain continuously monitors body temperature and quickly sends signals to regulate the temperate to cool down (through radiation, conduction, and convection and evaporation of perspiration) or heat up (vasoconstriction to decrease the flow of heat to the skin, cessation of sweating, shivering to increase heat production in the muscles, secretion of norepinephrine, epinephrine, and thyroxine to increase heat production). If we tried to control body temperature in the way we often try to prevent risks in organizations, it might look something like this: we'd all walk around in space suits heated to the perfect temperature, and we wouldn't be allowed to walk too quickly or too slowly. We'd also end up with control, but at the cost of losing much of our freedom to maneuver.

Now, for some rare cases where we can't self-correct quickly enough and the risks are particularly high, we might want to keep some form of up-front control. Say we have a peer-based budgeting process that no longer gets "approved" by an executive committee. But perhaps it's healthy, when it comes to signing actual checks with the bank for large amounts, to keep a mechanism where any large check must be signed by two people or more, or by a person holding a certain role, to reduce the risk that one rogue fool can put the organization at risk.

20

Peter Koenig, an astute observer of organizational life, talks about this role as the "source," the individual who has an intimate connection with an "information channel" to the purpose.

In his observations, which seem to be validated by hundreds of workshops he has run, in any organization there is a primary source. While the data is too scarce to make any definite assertions if this is true even of self-managing organizations, my impression is that it might be the case as well.

Let's avoid any misunderstanding (if you read this from an egalitarian-Green perspective, you might already be up in arms): this is not a way to reintroduce a power hierarchy, but a recognition that there might be a natural hierarchy at play. When people like Jos de Blok, Zobrist, or Chris Rufer share an intuition of where things might be heading, their colleagues tend to listen carefully, because they recognize their power to sense and articulate a vision for the future.

Koenig highlights the importance for the person acting as source to learn to materialize a heartfelt, creative vision, rather than a vision rooted in their personal ego. When this is done well, colleagues tend to embrace the source's vision because it feels true and right. The same principles apply to the many founder/sources of other initiatives which realize parts of the overall vision. Koenig suggests that if we map out the various initiatives within a self-managing organization over time from the founding moment, they will seem to unfold in a well-defined order rather like a tree with branches and twigs, i.e., in the form of a natural, creative hierarchy.

What is new in self-managing organizations is that the "CEO/source" can't impose his or her vision (he or she uses the advice for decision-making). The second difference: everyone else feels invited to sense and articulate in just the same way. While the founder/CEO might be a particularly powerful and respected source, everyone knows they have the power to act on what they sense needs to happen.

21

Skype conversation with the author, March 14, 2013.

22

This is the title of a poetic and in many ways prophetic book by Margaret J. Wheatley and Myron Kellner-Rogers. Published in 1998, it muses on what organizations and work might be like if we stopped thinking of organizations as machines and instead viewed them truly as living organisms. It's an extraordinary testament to the power of metaphors—and to the insights of the authors—that almost all of the insights I discovered during my research were suggested in Wheatley's and Kellner-Rogers' prose.

A warm

It's a joy to work with people one likes and, on top of that, admires for the quality of their work. Rarely, if ever, have I collaborated in a way that was as effortless and stimulating as it was with you, Etienne. The moments where I would look at a new batch of illustrations you sent were always thrilling, as I knew that some of them would utterly amaze me again and bring to life a complex thought with one visual stroke of genius. Oh, would I like to have this gift of yours!

Thank you, Isabelle (Normand), for suggesting that my book really needed a couple of illustrations, and for insisting that I should get to know Etienne who would be just the right person for it. Cécile and Martin, our collaboration ended on a strange and sad note, and yet I'm still grateful for your contribution, in particular for talking me out of the square format I had imagined for the book at first. Véronique (Geubelle), you stepped in when the book was almost ready and suddenly in need of a graphic designer on the shortest of notice. You've been a real savior. Betsy (Goolsby), your eagle eyes have saved this book from more errors and typos than I care to admit. It's been again a pleasure to work with you. As it has been with you, Lisa (Gill): thank you for your help with running the Indiegogo crowdfunding campaign, for collecting feedback on early drafts, and for the cheerful presence I've always felt in the background by my side throughout this project.

I also want to thank all of you who have mentioned and recommended the book *Reinventing Organizations* to others. Your word of mouth has helped what could have stayed an obscure, self-published book touch many, many lives and transform countless organizations. A warm thank you also for all of you who in some way have initiated or participated in the projects (audiobook, wiki, meetups, ...) that have sprung up around this topic.

Thank you also to all of you who have taken time to offer me feedback on draft versions of the book. You've helped me make my points more clearly and avoid potential misunderstandings: Alexandre Vandermeersch, Alix R. K. Farquhar, Charlotte Steenbergen, Cuan Mulligan, Eric Reynolds, Frank Widmayer, Gage Harris, Gary Henderson, Geert Acke, Gertraud Wegst, Heleen S. Kuiper, Helge Koops, Ian Yates, Jean de Limé, Johannes Terwitte, Jon Freeman, Kevin Buck, Klas Orsvärn, Lisa Gill, Mihai Popa-Radu, Monika de Neef, Nora Ganescu, Philippe Honigman, Reto Diezi, Sascha Kubiak, Tobias Wann, Tom Goubert, Vicky Ferrier, and Wannes Wilms.

I also want to go back to the beginnings and take my hat off to the founders and the employees of the trailblazing companies this book is based on. Your vision and your pioneering efforts are inspiring people all over the world to imagine a different future. What you've set out to do continues to fill me with awe.

In the book *Reinventing Organizations*, I thanked you, Raphaël and Noémie, for inviting me over and over again into your world of play, saving me often from my feverish drive to try and finish this book. And I thanked you, Hélène, for making everything in life more wonderful, including writing a book. I'm happy to report that good things can get better. It's such a privilege to be on a ride with you.

Frederic

thank you

A special "thank you" to all of you who have helped this book become a reality with your moral, as well as financial, support in crowdfunding this book! Feeling that there was a group of readers commited to this book and waiting for this book gave me a sense of community and spurred me on in the days when the writing or editing felt tedious.

A. Scirocco
Adam Darmstadt
Adelaida Manolescu
Adrienne Hall
AJ Stern
Alan Cyment
Albiez Olivier
Alec Marechal
Alex Vandermeersch
Alexander Jaeger
Alexander Koschke
Alia Z. Aurami
Alison Phillips
Alix R. K. Farquhar
Allison Pollard
Alvito de Souza
Amanda Sterling
Amon Woulfe
Ana Chirila
Ana Moreno Romero
Andrea Kuhfuss
Andrea Pro
Andreas Schaffron
Andrew Whittle
Anette Wallström
Ang Yi Hong
Anika Sauermann
Anita Ho
Anita Sheehan
Ann M. Pollock
Anne Bacheley

Anne Dassesse
Annelie Beller
Annemarie Schlack
Annette Gueth
Antje Koch Mahari
Antoine Decloedt
Antonio di Stefano
Arthur Guillome
Astrid Engelen
Barbara Wenk
Barry L. Lipscomb
Bart Kapteijns
Bart Van Bouwel
Beatrice Meulders
Benjamin Ancheta Jr.
Benoit Brassart
Benoit Charlet
Bernd Ankenbrand
Bertrand Michotte
Bettina Hartmann Bender
Biliana Sirakova
Birte Witteveen
Black Birds Three
Brandon Bayer
Brian Leclerc
Britta Tondock
Bronwen Morgan
Bruce Peters
C. Deiner-Karr
C. Randoing

Camero Ottens
Carl G. Shea
Carsten Direske
Carsten Steiner
Catherine Fraser
Catrin Yazdani
Celine Schillinger
Chang Shu Hao
Charlène Goulinet
Charles Grimes
Charles McFarland
Charles-Emmanuel Van Hecke
Charlotte Steenbergen
Chris Grieve
Chris Kempen
Chris Nerdal
Chris Walzer
Christian De Neef
Christian Hannel
Christian Keller
Dr. Christian Kemper
Dr. Christoph Bollig
Christoph Liebsch
Christoph Schlachte
Dr. Christopher Scholtz
Christopher Baan
Cian O'Byrne
Claire Le Grice
Claudia Scheidemann
Colleen Jamison

Corrine G. Lapinsky
Cuan Mulligan
D. Brands
D. Neeteson
D. Nouwens-Vermeulen
D. van Lith
Dan Händevik
Daniel Bartel
Daniel Hagman
Daniel S. Lee
Daniela Ogi
Dario Salice
Dariusz Klupi
Darran Trute
David Bruehlmeier
David Coombe
David J. Pecotic
David Jenkins
David Shriver
David Stuart
Dawid Stepien
Deborah Boyar
Deborah Cornick
Deborah Maarek
Delphine Roigt
Den Twan
Denis Morsomme
Dennis Perrin
Desnoeck Van Eeckhoutte
Dianne Dickerson

167

Diebrecht Hellofs
Diego Cuadra Leiva
Diego Lainez
Dieter Dehaes
Dieter Stößel
Dillon T. Kearns
Dirk Mattys
Djon Lind Andersen
Dmitry Buterin
Dominik Brüenner
Dominique Gibert
Donald Gilbert
Doug Shaw
Duc Ha Duong
Dunia Reverter
Edward B. Yarrish
Edwin Jansen
Eeva-Liisa Vihinen
Elf Coaching
Emily Macht
Emma Pugh
Enoch J. Cruz
Eric Legrand
Eric Platon
Eric Reynolds
Eric Theunis
Eskil Teigen
Eva Maria Schielein
Fabrice Aguilar
Fernando Cordova H.
Filip Lowette
Florian Halmburger
Franck Pralas
Frank Calberg
Frank Widmayer
Frederik Denkens
Fredrik Wessling
Freek Van Looveren
Freya C. Lustie
G. Sadlo
G.A. Been
Gabi Maier-Güttler
Gabor Veszi
Gabriel Melchert
Gage Harris
Gary Groesbeck

Gary Henderson
Geert Acke
Geert Cloostermans
Huwaert
Georg Meszaros
Georg Parlow
George Pór
Gertraud Wegst
Giampiero Bonifazi
Giovanni Quaratesi
Giulia Molinengo
Graham Boyd
Gudrun Vanderhaeghe
Guido Bosbach
H. van de Kraats
H. van Voorthuizen
Hani Boulos
Harry van der Velde
Heidi Gutekunst
Heidi Helfand
Heleen S. Kuiper
Helen Blässar
Helen Titchen Beeth
Helena Ruiz Fabra
Helge Koops
Howard Mason
Hugo Lopes
Ian Richardson
Ian Yates
Ilka Oevermann
Ina Gjikondi
Ivica Baraba
J. A. Thoms
J. David McGee
J. Kim Wright
J. L. Boniszewski
J. Nickel
J. W. Gruber
Jacek Wisniewski
James Denbow
Jan De Keyser
Jan-Paul Ouwerkerk
Janet Sanders
Jari Satka
Jasper De Rycker
JC de Jong

Jean de Limé
Jean-Claude Pierre
Jean-Paul Munsch
Jef Cumps
Joe Conte
Johan Magnusson
Johan Merckx
Johan Van den Bossche
Johan Verheven
Johann Entz-von
Zerssen
John Allen
John O'Brien
Joke Oosters
Jon Freeman
Jonas Johnsson
Jonathan Schreiber
Jordan M. Allen
Jørgen Lauge Sørensen
Joris Swinkels
Josh Usher
Joshua F. Dzielak
Joshua Greene
Jot McNeill
Jozeph Leendert
Minnaar
Juergen Schilling
Juha Usva
Julie Arts
Julie Boly
Justine Kenny
K. Gabriels
K. Gaynham
Kabir Kadre
Karen Van Garsse
Kathleen Jooris
Kathy Zirbser Zamba
Katia Van Belle
Katrien Rommens
Katrin Goecke
Kelley Harris
Ken Everett
Kevin Brunet
Kevin Buck
Kevin M.Ulug
Kim Oosvogels

Klas Orsvärn
Klaus Haasis
Koen Cuyckens
Koen De Herdt
Kristina Barisic
Kurt Specht
L. Kooistra
Langmar Peter
Leanne Libert
Liane Munro
Liberto Pereda
Linda Ford
Lisa Buddemeier
Lisa Clément
Lisa Gill
Lisbet Alfonso
Luke Madera
Luz Iglesias
Lynda Moe
Lyndon Rego
M. Scapens
M. Steeneveld
Malchus Kern
Manu Ganji
Mara Callaert
Marc Buckley
Marcel Altherr
Marcia Hyatt
Marco Jakob
Marcos H. N. Salles
Marcus A. Snyder
Marcus Pietrzak
Marcus Wermuth
Maria Begona Sampedro
Mariam Talakhadze
Marianne Urmes
Marie Peil
Marie-Pierre Le Cann
Mariël van der Linden
Mario Solana
Marita Schermer
Mark Kater
Markus Weigl
Martin Leitner
Mary Johnson
Maryse Lepage

Massimo Bau
Mate Szuecs
Mathias Weitbrecht
Mattias Hansson
Maureen McKenna
Maureen Van Overliw
Max Bindi
Max Blaauwbroek
Maya Shendelman
Meliha Dzirlo-Ayvaz
Michael Buergi
Michael J. Ross
Michael Paone
Michael Stern
Michael Tomoff
Michaela Schweitzer
Miet Vanhassel
Mihai Popa-Radu
Mike Munro Turner
Milton Georgo
Mireya Vargas
Monika de Neef
Nadine Nobile
Narayan D. C. Silva
Natalia Blagoeva
Neil Harris
Nial O'Reilly
Nic Woodthorpe-Wright
Nicola K. Kriesel
Nicolas Hennion
Niels Nijs
Nigel Pugh
Niklas Talling
Nikos Batsios
Nina Leonhard
Nora Ganescu
Ole Vilstrup Møller
Oliver Arnold
P. De Morree
P. Ola Jannhov
Paddy Baxter
Panu-Petteri
Leppäniemi
Pascale De Pré
Patrick Van Der Voorn
Paul Baecher

Paul Buysens
Paul Deneyer
Paul-Georges Crismer
Paula Penttinen
Per Hallager
Perry Timms
Pete Holliday
Peter Burns
Peter Comrie
Peter Green
Peter Oskam
Peter van Hecke
Philippe Henrotaux
Philippe Honigman
Philippe Renggli
Philippine Linn
Pierre Houben
Prasanth Menon
Quentin Kushner
Rafael Altavini
Rain Öpik
Rainer Wett
Ralf Metz
Randy Schenkat
Raphaël Guilbert
Regina Byrne
Régis ROY
Reinoud van Oirschot
Renate van Der Veen
Rene Korenromp
Rense Roet
Richard Andrews
Richard D. Bartlett
Richard Geer
Rik Verbeemen
Robin B. van Dalen
Rodrigo Silva Ortuzar
Roland Sterk
Roman Hagmann
Roman Risken
Rosemie
Vanwynsberghe
Ross Brandli
Ross Ferguson
Ruth Stoffel Kauflin
Ryan Unger

S. Unck
Sabine Haine
Sahar Asgharzadeh
Salvador Rodriguez
Samuel Troll
Sandra C. Kramer
Sara Cohen
Sarah C. Laughton
Sarah Clark
Sarah E. Cowley
Sascha Kubiak
Scott H. Sorvaag
Sebastian Dietz
Sébastien Piasco
Sergi Mora
Sergio Andreozzi
Shao-Chen
Sicco Maathuis
Silvia Seibert
Simon Berg
Simon Grossen
Simon Kranzer
Sinnay Sumac
Sivi Uitto
Stefan Faatz
Stefan Fischer
Stefan Groenendal
Steffen Grell
Stephane Dept
Stéphane Vuadens
Stéphane Witzmann
Stephen Starkey
Steve Thorp
Stuart J. Voaden
Stuart Whyte
Suchitra Davies-Webb
Susan Basterfield
Tacito V. Nobre
Tadhg MacCarthy
Taez Khan
Takeshi Yoshida
Tatiana Hendrix
The team of LastMason
Thea Carlson
Thibault Truyeb
Thierry Gauthron

Thierry Lepesant
Thomas Feichtinger
Thomas Perret
Thomas R. Christensen
Tiffanie J. Hunt-Mark
Tim Neugebauer
Tim Petricola
Tim Strasser
Tim Weinert
Timothy James Clark
Timothy L. Schsuter
Timothy Masson
Tobias Kuehnen
Tobias Wann
Tom Goubert
Tom Holt
Tom van Baarle
Tomé Ribeiro
Torben Lohmueller
Toria Thompson
Tory Gattis
Turid Mastenbroek
Ulrich Gerndt
Una Nicholson
Valerie Schlegel Stettler
Van Tran
Vasco Gaspar
Vellacott Thomas
Verena Hirschmann
Veronica M. Clifford
Veronique Janssens
Veronique Mino
Vicky Ferrier
Victoria Tiller
Vincent De Waele
Wannes Wilms
Wiebke Herding
Wim Focquet
Wolfgang Berger
Xiaohua Le
Yana Gebhardt
Yee Won Chong
Yeri Tiete
Yolande Demirian

reinventing organisations